Minute
Meditations™
for Healing
& Hope

Minute
Meditations™
for Healing
& Hope

EMILIE BARNES

HARVEST HOUSE PUBLISHERS

EUGENE, OREGON

MINUTE MEDITATIONS™ FOR HEALING & HOPE
Copyright © 2003 by Emilie Barnes
Published by Harvest House Publishers
Eugene, Oregon 97402
www.harvesthousepublishers.com

Library of Congress Cataloging-in-Publication Data
Barnes, Emilie, 1938–
    Minute meditations for healing and hope / Emilie Barnes.
        p. cm.
    ISBN 0-7369-1090-5
    1. Suffering—Prayer-books and devotions—English. 2. Consolation. I. Barnes, Emilie.
II. Title.
    BV4909 .B374 2003
    242'.4—dc21   2002014595

Printed in the United States of America

03 04 05 06 07 08 09 10 / BP-CF / 10 9 8 7 6 5 4 3 2

To My Dear Ones...

- ❧ Brad, my "soul son." You cheered me on with "You can do it, Mom." And I did.

- ❧ Jenny, my precious one. Our deepening relationship has been one of the Lord's great gifts during my illness.

- ❧ Bill, our new "son-in-love." You chose to embrace a family as well as a wife.

- ❧ Christine, Chad, Bevan, Bradley Joe, and Weston, my wonderful grandchildren. Thank you for your prayers, your beautiful smiles, your cute notes and pictures, and especially your warm hugs that gave me strength. You are a big part of your Grammy's healing.

- ❧ And, of course, my Bob—my sweetheart, partner, and hero. I know so much more about God because of the ways you show love to me.

To friends old and new, friends close by and far away. You brought me strawberries, rubbed my feet, wept with me, and even cleaned up after me. Best of all, you carried me with your prayers. Without your love and support, I would never have made it.

To the doctors, nurses, and staff of Hoag Cancer Clinic in Newport Beach, California, and the Fred Hutchinson Cancer Research Center in Seattle, Washington. You thought you were just doing your job, but I see you for what you are—living instruments of God's grace and healing.

And finally, to Dan Raponi, my bone marrow donor and my brother in Christ. You didn't pass up the opportunity to save a life. Not to be corny, I thank you from the very marrow of my being— and so do my family and friends. You'll be a part of everything the Lord accomplishes through me in the future.

A Note from Emilie

I've written this book to be an encouragement to all those who are walking through a difficult time in their lives. The cause could be an illness, the loss of a loved one, a divorce, or a financial downfall. My meditations are for both men and women as they wander through the valley of darkness. When my life looks down, I've learned to look upward. May these spiritual inspirations help ease your pain. May God's wisdom set your feet on solid ground and give you hope for tomorrow. Don't let your yesterdays ruin your todays.

You don't have to start at the beginning of this book. You can skip around and choose the reading that seems most suited for the day ahead. At the top of each page you will see three boxes. Each time you read a meditation, put a check mark in one of the boxes. This way you can keep track of those selections you have already read.

The prayer accompanying each reading will help you get started. Once you feel comfortable creating your own conversation with God, I would encourage you to pray with your own words. Some women I know choose to journal their prayers as a way to record their time spent with the Lord. You also might find this practice useful.

Each meditation closes with a recommended action that can help you implement in your life what you've read. May you feel the comfort of God's loving arms around you as you spend time in His word.

Emilie

Introduction

These devotions came about after thinking through my experience with mantel cell lymphoma (a non-Hodgkin's form of cancer).

When my first doctor gave me the news of my blood test, I was shocked and angered by the news. Fortunately, my Bob was present, and he was my rock! He held my hand and assured me that he would walk step-by-step with me. He would not leave me or forsake me; he would honor our marriage vows, which he had uttered those 41 years previous: "I will love you in sickness and in health, till death do us part."

That was the beginning of a nine-month process of trying to figure out the best treatment program for me. However, after those long, wasted nine months, we knew we had to get a second opinion. Several of our friends from a previous church told us about a prominent oncologist in Newport Beach, California. We made an appointment with him, brought all our records to him, and anxiously waited for him to agree with our first doctor's diagnosis. Instead, he was furious because I had not been treated professionally. Upon his initial examination, he found a large tumor in my stomach (of which we had never been told), my lymph glands were swollen throughout my body, and I had not received any treatment for the advanced stage of my disease.

He immediately started me on a strong dosage of chemotherapy and made an appointment with a radiologist to begin a very difficult radiation procedure.

After many months of intense prayer, both personally and collectively by our friends, and with the help and professional care of our medical team, my cancer went into remission. Unfortunately, the remission lasted only a short time. After consulting many specialists our doctor recommended that we consider a non-related bone-marrow transplant at Seattle's Fred Hutchinson Cancer Research Clinic.

In May of 2000, we left our home and checked into the "Hutch." We didn't realize what we would experience for the next five months. Through the bone-marrow donor bank in Minnesota, the staff identified one 23-year-old Canadian man who was willing to donate his bone marrow to be used in my transplant. I was overwhelmed that someone I didn't even know would step forward and be willing to sacrificially endure the painful procedure of having the bone marrow extracted from his hip so it could be transfused into my body. In all the samples in the donor's bank, only one person in the whole world matched my profile.

In June of 2000, at the University of Washington's Hospital, I went through a five-hour infusion of this precious young man's marrow into my body, not knowing how my body would receive his contribution. For the next 100 days, I was on a very rigid routine of specific medications and daily blood draws. The staff at the Hutch was incredible throughout the ordeal. They did whatever they could to make my stay as pleasant as possible.

We had the opportunity to meet other patients and their families from all over the world. What great stories of encouragement were they for us! Collectively, we became family. When one cried, we all cried; when one laughed, we all laughed. The Hutch became our world. Our lives as we knew them came to a halt, and we were captive to our disease.

After 125 days, we were released to go back home to our doctors' care. I thought that when I was able to go home, I would be totally well and ready to pick up where I left off. Not true! I still had many months of follow-up care with my hometown oncology staff. My body wanted to reject this foreign object called "an unrelated bone-marrow transplant." In order to not reject this new insert, my immune system had to be suppressed by large dosages of medication. My present stage of treatment is going very well. Tests show that I have 100 percent of the donor's bone marrow. I've had the opportunity to talk to this young man over the phone. What a precious time that has been!

Within a few months, I will travel back to Seattle for my two-year checkup. At that time I'm hoping that some of my medications can be reduced. I'm still claiming my theme verse, John 11:4, which states, "This sickness is not unto death, but for the glory of God, that the Son of God may be glorified by it" (NASB).

This book has been written so that you, the reader, will be encouraged by my reflections regarding one's journey through difficult times. Even though my experience has been cancer-related, these meditations can be helpful for anyone going through a difficult time.

I have found that those of us who have faith, prayer support, and personal assurance of answered prayer have a better chance of recovery than those who have no hope in spiritual strength. Even the medical staff testifies that patients who believe in God have a better chance of recovery than those who have no hope.

I trust that these thoughts will be enriching to you and you will be encouraged daily by the truths and principles you meditate upon.

I did not just want to be healed; I wanted everyone around me to know that my God would be glorified and that His Son would be lifted up. I strongly believe that I am alive today because of God, my doctors, and the medications that have been developed for my disease. I trust that you will be lifted up as you read these devotions.

Read His Word

Do not let them (words) depart from your sight;
keep them (words) in the midst of your hearts.
For they are life to those who find them,
and health to all their whole body.

—Proverbs 4:21-22 NASB

've realized that God gives me life and health as I open my heart to His Word. Make a daily practice of reading God's Word. The time of day or location don't matter. Jesus prayed at various times and various places. Your desire to pray is what counts. There's something about an illness that makes God's words so very precious. His thoughts are so much higher than our thoughts and His ways are so much higher than our ways. Use this time to get to know Him in a way you have never known Him before. Sometimes I was so sick and weak I couldn't read. Those were the days when Bob would read to me from the Psalms and Proverbs. What special memories I have of those occasions. They were sweet as honey.

Now that I'm up and about I have a special prayer closet where I go each day to spend precious time praying, reading, and meditating on His Word.

Prayer: *Father God, give me the desire to come to You each day and read a portion of Your Word. If I'm too sick, let me ask someone to read to me. Amen.*

Action: Start today to read God's Word. Start with the book of John and then enjoy portions of Psalms and Proverbs.

Reflections:

Control Anger

🌿

If you are angry, don't sin by nursing your grudge.
Don't let the sun go down with you still angry—
get over it quickly; for when you are angry
you give a mighty foothold to the devil.

—EPHESIANS 4:26-27

Oh yes, there were times when I was angry at God. I couldn't understand this thing called cancer. Why do I have to have it? What causes it? Can it be cured? Through all these testings of my faith, I came to a better understanding of life. What is life? How do I get involved? What part do I play in life? Even though I was angry, I never turned it into sin. I never cursed God, never gave up on Him as my God, and never lost trust in Him as my strength and my shield. God didn't get smaller. In fact, He became bigger than ever.

I realized kind words build up and negative words tear down. I found I was able to have better days when I protected my thought process than when negative thoughts filled my mind. Satan was not to gain victory over me during this illness. I knew that God did not give me cancer. But since the germs of the fallen world permitted my body to contract this disease, I was going to make the best of it and God was going to gain the glory.

Prayer: *Father God, You have given me the power to reject all anger. Today I decide not to get angry and sin.*

I will keep Your name holy, and Satan will not separate me from Your love. Amen.

Action: Today I decide not to sin with my anger. I decide to think, speak, and act positively.

Reflections:

Live for Today

May the God of hope fill you with all joy
and peace as you trust in him,
so that you may overflow with hope…

—ROMANS 15:13 NIV

As I've observed my five grandchildren over the years, one thing stands out very vividly: their ability to live and enjoy the moment. They can take the "now" and make it a gift. I'm trying to forget about what happened yesterday and what might happen tomorrow and just experience the fullness of today.

In order to capture the present, we need to give less attention to worries, mistakes, what's going wrong, general concerns, things to get done, the past, the future, and the undone. *Today I will only think about today. No regrets for the past or fears about the future.* When you do this, all your focus is on the now. You can smile, laugh, pray, think, and enjoy what each moment brings.

Often our anxieties are about situations we have no control over. I tell the ladies at my seminars that 85 percent of the things we worry about never happen. Why spend all that negative energy on something that probably will never occur?

We are to stop and smell the roses, hear the train whistle, see the puffy clouds in the sky, hear the rain fall, and watch the snow flurries. When we begin to see and experience every minute, we will also begin to see the grandeur of God and His vastness.

Prayer: *Father God, let me learn to live for the now. I truly want to observe all that You have given me. Amen.*

Action: Buy, taste, and enjoy an ice cream cone.

Reflections:

Check Your Power Source

*The Lord says, "I will make my people strong
with power from me!...Wherever they go
they will be under my personal care.*

—ZECHARIAH 10:12

In Southern California, we have many service companies that want to take care of our every need. We have personal trainers, personal shoppers, home decorators, personal groomers, valet parking, and personal guides at Disneyland. However, none of these services can take care of our spiritual needs. We need someone much larger in life than a service provider.

Since God has promised to make us strong with His power, we need to break out and take some control over our lives. God has given us many truths that enable us to make appropriate choices for proper and healthy living.

When we are confronted with certain illnesses, we must rely on good common sense. Your intuition will give you insight on what needs to be done.

Remember that God is always there looking over your shoulder. When He is needed, He is there! You are under His personal care at all times.

Prayer: Father God, let me rely on Your power more. The
weight that I'm presently carrying is too heavy.
Help me to say no when I find myself trying to
solve all my problems. Amen.

Action: Go to God in prayer for your decisions.
Depend upon Him more each day. Step down
so He can step up.

Reflections:

Keep On Planting

*Keep on sowing your seed, for you never know
which will grow—perhaps it all will.*

—ECCLESIASTES 11:6

oday is a special day in my life. Two years ago, my Bob and I departed from our home in California to travel to Seattle, and begin a 125-day ordeal that included a bone-marrow transplant for my lymphoma disease. For three long years, I had been in treatment for my illness. Long sessions of chemotherapy and many radiation treatments could not keep me in remission. My wonderful oncologist, Dr. Barth, kept trying to make me well, but nothing worked for any length of time. I'd do great, and then I'd fall back. Back and forth, in and out.

But then Dr. Barth contacted the Fred Hutchinson Cancer Research Clinic in Seattle. They said they had a new protocol that might work for me. Of course, we said yes. Let's plant one more seed—who knows? This seed might sprout and bear fruit. Praise God—it has. I've been in remission for two years, and all tests show no signs of cancer. Soon I will return to Seattle for my two-year checkup. My encouragement to you is to keep on planting seeds. We never know which ones will produce fruit.

Prayer: Father God, You are the planter of all seeds. Thank
You for presenting the right conditions for my
seeds to grow. Amen.

Action: Keep planting new seeds.

Reflections:

Self-Talk

*How precious it is, Lord, to realize that you are
thinking about me constantly! I can't even count how
many times a day your thoughts turn toward me.*

—PSALM 139:17

Do you ever catch your thoughts taking a negative turn? As you check your self-talk, do you realize that a lot of junk is crossing your mind? Most of us are very good at criticizing ourselves. We find fault very easily.

I suggest that you develop a more positive thought process. When I know that God is thinking about me constantly, how can I not think positive of myself? If I am worthy to Him, why should I not be worthy to myself? As you look in the mirror of life, don't be afraid to say loud and clear, "good job." We aren't being conceited when we recognize the good in our life—however, we must recognize that all good comes from our heavenly Father.

Many times, after going through a delicate medical procedure, my Bob and I would celebrate by doing something special. Usually we didn't do anything big—just a recognition that I had done a "good job." Keep telling yourself the positive—don't let the negative take hold of your thought process.

Prayer: *Father God, knowing that You are thinking of me has often given me extra strength to carry on for another day. Your thoughts are precious to me! Amen.*

Action: Look in a mirror and say, "good job."

Reflections:

Number Our Days

---

*Teach us to number our days and recognize
how few they are; help us to spend them as we should.*

—PSALM 90:12

How often do we talk in terms of days? Usually our reference is in terms of years. He's 37 years old, they were married 15 years ago, I've not had a drink in 8 years, World War II was 63 years ago.

This verse suggests that we are to number our days. We are encouraged to live each day to the fullest so that when our life draws to an end, we have gained "a heart of wisdom" or spent each day as we should. When we live each day unto the Lord, we live it with gusto and enthusiasm for Him.

I have found that as I get older the inevitables of life happen and I must learn to adjust to the unknowns that appear from time to time. One cannot do this in years but only from day to day and often from hour to hour. Aging isn't a choice—it just happens. With each new pain and ache, don't become negative, but rather celebrate the life that God has given you. How we respond to these aches will determine how we grow old.

Prayer: Father God, I want to be realistic about the un-
              knowns that will attack my body. Please give me
              the proper attitude to accept these as a part of life.
              Amen.

Action: Celebrate the unknowns.

              Has He not said my strength is as my day?
              That He will wipe my every tear away?
              And that He's with me, come what may?

              Has He not said that water won't o'erflow?
              That He'll direct the path that I must go?
              And peace past understanding I may know?

              Has He not given a name on which to call?
              With angels charged to hold me lest I fall?
              And are not fervent prayers effectual?

              Will He not make my wilderness be glad?
              And not His blessings daily myriad?
              And is there not a balm in Gilead?

              Since Jesus is the Word exhibited,
              And with the precious Word I'm tenanted,
              May I not boldly speak what He has said?

                        —E. Ruth Glover

Reflections:

For Me to Live Is Christ

Even though the fig trees are all destroyed,
and there is neither blossom left nor fruit,
and though the olive crops all fail, and all the fields lie
barren; even if the flocks die in the fields and the
cattle barns are empty, yet I will rejoice in the Lord;
I will be happy in the God of my salvation.

—HABAKKUK 3:17-18

Many times, as we look back, we see that most of our possessions have faded away. Health becomes so precious when we no longer have it. Paul, in Philippians 1:21 (NIV), expresses it very well when he says, "For me, to live is Christ and to die is gain." Paul understood the ultimate principle for successful living. He realized that though our material possessions can be wonderful and enjoyable, the real joys that last forever are our steadfast trust and joy in the Lord. Through good times and bad times, through sick times and healthy times, through the up times and down times, we need to express joy—because God has saved us from our sins.

When I accepted this concept, I was able to give my disease to God and move on. I knew that I was in good medical and spiritual hands and that God wanted the best for me.

Prayer: *Father God, let me believe that for me to live is Christ and to die is gain. I want to be assured that I can live out this principle. Give me the power to accept it in my own life. Amen.*

Action: Begin to believe and live out, "For one to live is Christ and to die is gain."

Reflections:

Have the Right Perspective

You are my refuge and my shield,
and your promises are my only source of hope.

—PSALM 119:114

People have asked me how I can be so upbeat when so many things around me are negative. I guess it's because of my perspective on life. Through Scripture and life experiences, I have come to trust that God has a master plan for my life. He knew my beginning and He knows the events of my end. His words give me so much comfort. I have learned that I can count on His promises. When the psalmist tells me that God is my shield and that His promises are my only source of hope, I believe it. God's character is one of honor, trust, and reliability that I can bank on for my life.

God's Word brings me light on a foggy day, it brings me hope when I become discouraged, and it helps me not to make a mountain out of a molehill. His Word gives me the right perspective on life. I know my time on earth is such a short time and my time with Him after this earthly experience will be for eternity. I have conquered death through Christ—it has no sting; it is swallowed up in victory (1 Corinthians 15:54-56).

Prayer: *Father God, O how I cherish my eternal perspec-*
tive. I pray that all my friends can enjoy the peace
and comfort You give me daily. Amen.

Action: Stand encouraged in difficult times.

Reflections:

Receive His Peace

*May God our Father and the Lord Jesus Christ
give you all of his blessings
and great peace of heart and mind.*

—1 Corinthians 1:3

ord, for whatever I am receiving and about to receive—pain as well as joy—please teach me the secret of giving thanks for what I have already received, what has shaped my life in the past, and what is shaping me today. Please do not let my yesterdays spoil today. Please fill my life with thanksgiving. Let me reach out and encourage others who are in similar circumstances with the same comfort that You have bestowed on me.

❧ ❧ ❧

I can remember going to a doctor's appointment when I was nervous about a procedure that day or the results I was getting from a previous test. I didn't sleep well, I was anxious, I couldn't relax, my speech pattern was altered, my energy was zapped—I just couldn't find peace. Sometime during the morning routine of breakfast, devotions, and prayer, something was said that made me realize I was trying to solve the problem myself and not give the situation to the Lord. He is capable when I am not.

Prayer: Father God, You let me get myself in a dither. I get anxious and worried just to be reminded that I need You. I know that peace comes from You— when am I going to learn? Please be patient with me. Amen.

Action: When you become worried, take a deep breath, relax your shoulders, and utter a prayer toward God.

Reflections:

He Is Not Far Away

His purpose in all of this is that they should seek
after God, and perhaps feel their way toward him
and find him—though he is not far from any one of us.

—ACTS 17:27

The Lord is always there for you, waiting to fill your life with encouragement and affirmation, waiting mercifully to restore your soul. He does it through the words of Scripture, through the soft whisper of His Holy Spirit, and especially through the people who love, accept, and support you.

When I've felt that I'm not close to God, I realize that I'm the one who has moved away, not God. We can always step back into His presence by expressing our thanks to Him for all He has done for us.

Even though these are difficult days for us, I've found that there's always something to be thankful for: a nurse with a smile, a phone call from someone who is dear to me, medicine that is helping me get well, a doctor who gives me assurance that everything's going to be okay. God has little helpers everywhere who perform acts of encouragement for my hurting soul. I want to appreciate all that they do to encourage me each day.

Prayer: *Father God, I don't want You to go very far from me. I really need to know that You are close by. Your assurances mean a lot to me at this time. You are truly my strength during these difficult days. Amen.*

Action: Reach out to someone today and be an encouragement. Tell them where your peace comes from.

Reflections:

Let Your Roots Go Down

Let your roots grow down into him [God]
and draw up nourishment from him.
See that you go on growing in the Lord,
and become strong and vigorous in the truth
you were taught. Let your lives overflow with joy
and thanksgiving for all he has done.

—COLOSSIANS 2:7

When our roots grow deep in faith, we bear much fruit for the kingdom. You may wonder as I do, *How can my roots grow deep while I'm in the fight of my life?* In my earlier stages of treatment I may not have understood, but as I got further into my treatment, I learned how to let my roots grow deeper and faster. My heart longed, as a deer pants for water, to know God in a deeper way than I had ever known Him before.

Bob and I both love our garden. We know that during the heat of the summer we have to water our trees deeply. If we don't, they will not grow tall and strong. If we water sparingly, the roots stay near the surface and a slight breeze can topple the trees. If you want your trees to be formidable against the strong winds, they need to have roots that have grown deep down into the ground.

Prayer: Father God, let me take the time to allow my faith
              to grow down deep and draw nourishment from
              You. Amen.

Action: Let your life overflow with joy and thanks-
              giving for all He has done.

Reflections:

It's Your Choice

I have set before you life or death, blessing or curse.
Oh, that you would choose life;
that you and your children might live.

—Deuteronomy 30:19

There's something about an illness that makes us think about what's really important in life. It gives us the opportunity to ponder the *big* issues. For once, we don't take for granted anything. We also appreciate all the *little* things we used to take for granted, such as standing up, taking a walk, having a few moments without pain, a child's smile, keeping a good meal down, even a normal bowel movement (when you're on heavy medication, that's reason to shout).

I had to make many choices—some pleasant and some not so pleasant—on some days when I didn't want to make a choice. I would often defer that process to Bob. "Honey, you choose for me. I just can't." However, there is one choice I can't have someone else make, and that's the choice between life and death. I'm the only one who can do that. There is a choice between life and death—and it's ours to make. When we choose life, we will have victory over death. It's an eternal promise—when we die, we just go from earth to heaven.

Prayer: Father God, I am trusting You for a new season in
              my life. I am ready to begin again, and I need You
              to show me the way. Amen.

Action: Choose life today. Don't wait another day.
              Tomorrow might be too late.

Reflections:

□ □ □

ℋe Cares

Let him have all your worries and cares,
for he is always thinking about you
and watching everything that concerns you.

—1 PETER 5:7

ohn W. Peterson, the great Christian songwriter, wrote:

No one understands like Jesus, He's a friend beyond compare; meet Him at the throne of mercy, He is waiting for you there.

No one understands like Jesus, every woe He sees and feels; tenderly He whispers comfort, and the broken heart He heals.

No one understands like Jesus, when the foes of life assail, you should never be discouraged, Jesus cares and will not fail.

No one understands like Jesus, when you falter on the way, though you fail Him, sadly fail him, He will pardon you today.

The uplifting chorus after each verse sings:

No one understands like Jesus, when the days are dark and grim; no one is so near, so dear as Jesus. Cast your every care on Him.

We are not big enough or strong enough to carry all our worries. We need help, and Jesus is there to lighten our load. Without Him, I would have been crushed under the load—it was too heavy.

Prayer: *Father God, thank You that Your Spirit knows how to pray for us, even when we do not. I rely on Your Holy Spirit to make the depth of my heart known to You this day. Amen.*

Action: Give God all of your cares—*all*, not just a few.

Reflections:

God Has a Plan

🌿

It is God himself who has made us what we are
and given us new lives from Christ Jesus;
and long ages ago he planned that we should spend
these lives in helping others.

—EPHESIANS 2:10

Isn't it good to know we are His workmanship, planned long ago? We are His ongoing project that hopefully glorifies Him. What a comfort it is to know that we are just where God has planned for us to be. You might be asking, "Does God really want me to be under this burden of disease?" Not necessarily the disease, but He does want us in a situation where we can help others.

I can remember very vividly several couples in Seattle who mentioned, "I'm so glad you are here at the Hutch so you can offer me comfort." Bob would look at me and I at him, and we'd give a non-verbal glance that said, "If our disease was for that one person, it was worth it."

Now is the time in your life when you can give a hopeless patient hope. You may never have the same opportunity again. Your smile, your hug, your encouragement just might be what that person needs today. Step out and live life on purpose.

Prayer: Father God, I am thinking of several people I know that need my love. Let me follow through and share Your love with them. Give me courage to reach out and help a hurting world. Amen.

Action: Humble yourself before God and ask Him to show you the way.

Reflections:

Lord, Speak Out

🌱

Lord, you know all about it. Don't stay silent!
Don't desert me now! Rise up, O Lord my God...

—PSALM 35:22-23

h God, as You stand in heaven, I beg You to be stirred about my situation. I feel as though You have abandoned my every call. React to my pleading and don't desert me now! I need You today more than any other time in my life. My illness trembles when You come to my defense. Speak with a shouting voice and make my illness retreat to a manageable level.

🌱 🌱 🌱

Bob and I can vividly remember our continual petitions to God for help. We claimed every verse of Scripture that offered us assurance that God would hear us, but we still didn't feel like He was. Were we not strong enough in our vocal requests, were we wavering in our faith, was the disease really unto death? Why wasn't I getting any better?

I'm not sure when or why, but I could begin to see my body getting healthier. My CAT scans showed signs of remission, my blood counts were better. I didn't need any more hydration. Gradually, I could see that God was using the doctors, the medications, and His own touch to heal my body.

Prayer: Father God, thank You for not getting impatient with me. At times, I have so little faith and I don't trust You enough. Thank You for all You do for me. Amen.

Action: Continue to pray with vigor.

Reflections:

Do all the good you can
By all the means you can,
In all the ways you can,
In all the places you can,
At all the times you can,
To all the people you can,
As long as ever you can.

—JOHN WESLEY

Fear Not

I have called you by name; you are mine.
When you go through deep waters and great trouble,
I will be with you. When you walk through
rivers of difficulty, you will not drown!
When you go through the fire of oppression,
you will not be burned up—the flames will not
consume you. For I am the Lord your God...

—ISAIAH 43:1-3

Notice that Isaiah says "when," not "if." Sooner or later, all of us will go through deep troubles. If you aren't right at this moment, you eventually will. Stand in line—your time will come.

When we are young or when life is treating us so well, it is hard to think about the woes of life. They might happen to others, but surely not to me or my family. But if the Lord grants us an abundance of years, we will all experience the woes I'm in the midst of:

- ❧ passing through the deep waters

- ❧ wading through the rivers

- ❧ walking through the fire

During this time I find that:

- ❧ God is with me.

    ❧ The rivers aren't sweeping over me.

    ❧ The fires aren't burning me.

    ❧ God is calling me by name, and I will fear no evil.

Prayer: *Father God, teach me to pray. Move me to prayers. Grace me with the strength and resolve to make talking with You my highest priority. Amen.*

Action: Fear not, for He is your God.

Reflections:

His Name Has Honor

🌰

I worship, giving thanks to you for all your
lovingkindness and your faithfulness,
for your promises are backed by all the honor
of your name. When I pray, you answer me,
and encourage me by giving me the strength I need.

—PSALM 138:2-3

When someone promises me something, I want to know what backs up that promise. Does he have enough financial resources to make that pledge? Does he have the political power to make that promise? Has he been a man of honor who has lived up to his promises? Our honor is one of our most valuable possessions. It takes years to obtain but can be lost in a twinkle of an eye.

God has demonstrated His abiding character and His commitment to keep His promises. When He gives you a promise in His Word, you can take it to the bank. It's sealed with His honor.

As I have walked through my troublesome valley, I can definitely say that God has lived up to every promise. He has heard and answered my prayers. He has been my shield, He has been my protector, and He has given me peace beyond description. He has encouraged me by giving me the strength I needed for the occasion.

Prayer: Father God, You are the God of every moment.
Teach me to order my ways even as You direct my
paths. Thank You for Your instructive presence
in my life.

Action: Step out in faith and trust that you can
depend on God.

Reflections:

Be a Person of Character

❧

Be beautiful inside, in your hearts,
with the lasting charm of a gentle and quiet spirit
which is so precious to God.

—1 Peter 3:4

Men and women spend millions and millions of dollars each year trying to make themselves more attractive (yes, even men are buying cosmetics). When I go by the cosmetic counter at my favorite department store, the ladies gather around the beauty consultant as if they're at McDonald's in line for a hamburger, drink, and fries. Even in economic downturns, people continue to buy cosmetics. We all want to be beautiful on the outside. Improving our outward beauty is one thing; improving our inward beauty is far more difficult.

I have the privilege of knowing some very godly women who model their inward beauty to me. They are wonderful ladies to be around. They adorn themselves with a gentle and quiet spirit which is pleasing to the Lord. As I grow older, I want to be more lovely inside, keeping in mind that growing older brings me closer to my Lord.

Even though we are going through difficult days, we can still radiate our inner beauty. Don't slide into the rut of being an ugly complainer. We can still be charming, even in a very difficult situation.

Prayer: *Father God, will things ever be right again? I am broken, and healing seems a long way off. I know Your promises are true. I need Your grace to believe. Amen.*

Action: I am going to have a quiet spirit today.

Reflections:

God's Timetable

❧

There is an appointed time for everything.
And there is a time for every event under heaven…
He has made everything appropriate in its time.

—ECCLESIASTES 3:1,11 NASB

ne great accomplishment in life is learning to find rest in our appointed time—relishing the joys and challenges that come with each new stage of living. These include the excitement and possibilities of youth, the satisfaction and fulfillment of maturity, and the wisdom and patience of later years. As we advance in age, though we see our youth and its aspirations flee by, we gather wonderful memories to cherish and new lessons to learn. We anticipate, more and more eagerly, the time of being with the Lord for eternity.

I have learned that God has a master plan for my life, and I am comforted in knowing I live by His timetable. I have already experienced so many of His seasons—each one good in its own way. Why shouldn't I expect the next stage to be good as well?

God is the potter and I am the clay. He will mold me and make me in His own way. Remain pliable and flexible so God can mold you more easily.

Prayer: Father God, You are my friend. I know that You work all things together for my good. Help me be more flexible. Amen.

Action: In your journal, write down five memories you are thankful for.

Reflections:

Because the Lord is my Shepherd,
I have everything I need!
He lets me rest in the meadow grass
and leads me beside the quiet streams.
He restores my failing health.
He helps me do what honors him the most.
Even when walking through the dark valley of death
I will not be afraid, for you are close beside me,
guarding, guiding all the way.
You provide delicious food for me
in the presence of my enemies.
You have welcomed me as your guest;
blessings overflow!
Your goodness and unfailing kindness shall
be with me all my life,
and afterwards I will live with you
forever in your home.

—PSALM 23

Be a Sower
of Seeds

Yes, I am the Vine; you are the branches.
Whoever lives in me and I in him
shall produce a large crop of fruit.
For apart from me you can't do a thing.

—JOHN 15:5

A smart woman once told me that a wise person does in her youth what a fool does in her old age. Let's not wait until we are old to do what we should have done when we were young.

It is a well-known (and biblical) principle: Whatever we sow, we reap. The harvest always comes after the planting. All other things being equal, we can anticipate that with good weather and adequate rain, we will have a large crop—if we have made the effort to sow in the first place. In a sense, I am experiencing a harvest time in my life right now. I am reaping the results of friendship seeds sown in other seasons. I remember busy times when I almost didn't have time for friends—when a phone call, or a note, or a luncheon date, or even a word of prayer was truly a sacrifice of my time, when making time for others was truly a struggle.

How glad I am that I made those efforts to sow seeds of friendship and love and to cultivate those crops carefully. Now I have the privilege of reaping an abundant harvest. I am so blessed to have all my family, friends, and loved ones around me during this time in my life. Through their expressions of love and kindness, they have shared Christ with me.

Prayer: *Father God, help me today to keep my heart and mind focused on You, Your goodness, and Your blessing in my life. Amen.*

Action: Express your love and kindness to someone today—with a phone call, a note, or in person!

Reflections:

A Great Return

*May he multiply you a thousand times more,
and bless you as he promised.*

—DEUTERONOMY 1:11

To know that my blessings will be increased a thousand times is almost beyond comprehension. After all, a bank might give me 3 percent interest on my savings, but a 1000 percent markup is simply unbelievable. Yet this is exactly what I am promised in this scripture. The Lord has promised to increase my blessings—and your blessings—a thousandfold! Wow!

Of course, this verse is talking about more than money or possessions. It's also talking about a return on investment in family, emotional stability, marriage, health, desires, and all other components of life. And it doesn't have a time limit, either. Perhaps some of the blessing I'm promised will happen in eternity and in the lives of those who come after me on this earth.

Still, I know that God keeps His promises—and what a promise this is! Knowing my blessings are growing and growing and growing gives me strength—even amid the uncertainties of my physical health.

Prayer: Father God, sometimes I am discouraged by the "dailiness" of life. Calm me today, Father. Help me to set my sights on things above and give You thanks. Amen.

Action: Give someone a blessing today.

Reflections:

Joy Comes in the Morning

Weeping may go on all night,
but in the morning there is joy.

—PSALM 30:5

ears, for me, have been so cleansing. My pillow was soaked sometimes by all my discouragements during this ordeal. While you are on this journey, tears help you to be transparent to yourself, your mate, your family, and the world. My Bob has been so great during our ordeal. At times, the caregiver has a tougher time than the patient. When I get weepy, he is always there to soothe and comfort me. He knows I don't need any answers from him, just support.

It's okay to cry—don't try to hide it. Be real; your illness is real. The people around you need to know that illnesses are real. That's one of the blessings of an illness. It takes away all of the phoniness of life. You become very real. The more real you are, the better those around you will respond. Be open with your conversations. Children, depending on their ages, don't always need to know everything. However, they need to be aware that life is difficult for you at the moment.

For me, after each cry, the morning reflected the joy of Jesus. His promises were more real and I realized more than ever His love for me.

Prayer: *Father God, let me be brave even when tears flow from my heart. Let me know that it's okay to cry. Please give me joy in the morning. Amen.*

Action: Look for joy in the morning.

Reflections:

Have Pleasant Dreams

You can sleep without fear; you need not be afraid
of disaster or the plots of wicked men,
for the Lord is with you; he protects you.

—Proverbs 3:24-26

o you ever have trouble sleeping? Then claim this promise. I know there can be plenty of nights that you might toss and turn. You just can't relax from thinking about tomorrow's schedule. You've got to do this and you've got to do that. When will it end? All the tests, one specialist after another, a change of medication—I can't seem to keep track of it all. Is it taken in the morning, at noon, at dinner, or just before I go to bed? Wow! There's a lot to be concerned about. However, this verse tells me that I can lie down without fear and even have pleasant dreams.

You don't have to count sheep to fall asleep. Just remember that God knows all about your tomorrows. He has gone ahead of you to smooth out the rough patches. No information from any test comes to you first. He has already heard and approved of it before you are told. If He takes care of you today, He will certainly take care of you tomorrow. Lay your head on the pillow and know He will protect you from all harm. Night-night!

Prayer: Father God, I want to be content with whatever
You choose to provide. Give me the grace to let the
rest go and trust You for my every need. Amen.

Action: Trust the Lord that you will have pleasant
sleep and will enjoy your dreams.

Reflections:

He has not promised we will never feel lonely,
But He has promised that in Him
We will never be alone.

He has not promised that we will be free
From pain and sorrow,
But He has promised He will be our help,
Our strength, our everlasting peace.

No matter what happens in our lives,
We can believe fully in His promise…
We can rest confidently in His love.

—AUTHOR UNKNOWN

Sing Confident Praises

O God, my heart is quiet and confident.
No wonder I can sing your praises!

—PSALM 57:7

ut God, You must not understand my situation. See I've got this and that disease and I've got this and that to do. Do you really expect me to be quiet, to be confident, and to sing your praises? I can't do that; I've got too many problems.

Because we have problems, we must be quiet, be confident, and sing praises.

A famous old violin maker always made his instruments out of wood from the north side of the tree. Why? Because the wood which had endured the brunt of the fierce wind, icy snow, and raging storm lent a finer tone to the violin. Trouble and sorrow give the soul its sweetest melodies.

One whose security is in God can be steadfast and unmovable at all times and in any situation. When life seems to crash upon you, you can say, "My soul is bowed down, but my heart is fixed." When we have this security and stability, we can sing a precious song of victory.

Yes, God does know our situation. It is easy to sing when the days are bright, but a steadfast heart can also sing in times of trouble.

Prayer: Father God, my light feels a bit dim today, but I come to You, the Light of the World. Light Your fire within me once again, that I might shine for You. Amen.

Action: Sing a song of praise.

Reflections:

You Will Smile Again

Oh my soul, why be so gloomy
and discouraged? Trust in God!
I shall again praise him for his wondrous help;
he will make me smile again, for he is my God!

—PSALM 43:5

get so upset when I don't act like a spiritual person! I know what I should do, but....

There were times when I didn't think I would smile or laugh again. This verse helped me to remember, "He will make me smile again." Don't you just love that? When my spirit becomes gloomy, I choose to continually trust in God. Christ does not force our will; He only receives what we give Him.

Despite what's happening in our lives, we can say loud and clear, "We will not fear!" Time and time again, God has given me confidence that I can believe Him for the future. He is our refuge and strength. Pretty simple, isn't it?

Quite often now, I catch a smile coming across my face. It feels so good to smile. Smiling is one of the most therapeutic exercises we can do. Sick people aren't expected to smile, but I do, and that astonishes my friends. A smile reflects the confidence we have in our Lord. We trust Him enough to reflect a sign of joy—a big bright smile.

Prayer: Father God, grant me the desire to smile. I love to share a smile with others, and I love to receive one back. May others see You through my smile. Amen.

Action: Don't forget to smile.

Reflections:

My deafness forces me to depend on God more
so that I can hear through Him.
He brought me peace and taught me
how to overcome my deafness.

—HEATHER WHITESTONE
MISS AMERICA, 1995

Give Love Away

🍂

Love is patient, love is kind....
Love does not delight in evil but rejoices
with the truth. It always protects, always trusts,
always hopes, always perserveres.

—1 CORINTHIANS 13:4,6-7 NIV

In spite of illness, one can remain productive by reflecting the love that God has given us through His Son, Jesus. In sickness, we have the opportunity to learn patience and kindness.

In God's love, I have found Him always there to protect, to help me trust, and to provide hope. In turn, I'm able to persevere through it all. I have learned God's megatruths by experiencing this illness. God has surrounded me with people who really love me for who I am and not for what I can do.

Love is the greatest gift of all. Someone you encounter today will need a little bit of love. Make this a special day for them—love them. In turn, you will also be loved. You have to empty your cup before you are able to take in more. I've learned when I give away my life, I receive new life.

Prayer: Father God, oh just to rest in Your presence for a
moment or two. So many things to do, places to
be. I want to be with You in it all, dear Lord.
Come—I welcome Your presence. Amen.

Action: Give away your love today.

Reflections:

□ □ □

Spring Is Here

For the winter is past, the rain is over and gone.
The flowers are springing up and the time
of the singing of birds has come. Yes, spring is here.

—SONG OF SOLOMON 2:11-12

I so look forward to getting past the winter rains of life. I live for the day when I can return to a normal lifestyle—enjoying church, sporting events, and restaurants; eating a green salad, playing with a gathering of small children. It seems so long since I've seen the budding of spring flowers or heard the chirping of new songbirds. The other day, as Bob was driving me to the clinic, we passed a Starbucks and he said, "Won't it be good to be able to stop and have a leisurely cup of coffee?" At the time, it seemed so far away.

I have come to realize there are various seasons of one's life, and I can assure you that these last few months have not been easy on me or my family and friends. Everyone has been wonderful during this season of life. They have come alongside, assuring me that spring will come and I will join in the celebration. Come on, spring, I can't wait for you to arrive!

Prayer: *Father God, thank You for the blessing of my*
family and friends. Touch each life today. Draw

them closer to You. This is my heart's prayer for those I love.

Action: When spring arrives, plant some flower seeds!

Reflections:

Be Content

I have learned to be content
whatever the circumstances.

—Philippians 4:11 NIV

ut Lord, I thought this detour was only going to be a mile or two, I didn't sign up for a 10-K run—I didn't realize it was going to be for years. This road has been bumpy with deep ruts and a lot of dust flying in my face. I haven't always enjoyed the long waits while the big trucks go by. It seems like it's always hurry up and wait.

But now, I'm beginning to enjoy the road and things don't look so bad. In fact, I've met some wonderful people along the way. We've even shared some picnic lunches and relaxed in the shade of a large sycamore tree.

It's hard to be inconvenienced, but each time it happens, I'm learning to accept all that comes my way. Now I can understand this detour in my life better. Some wise person once said, "If you're not content with what you have, you'll never be content with what you want."

Prayer: *Father God, You instructed Your people to prepare for what was to come. Grant me Your wisdom and grace to hear Your voice and consider my ways before You. Amen.*

Action: Be content for today.

Reflections:

If Only...

*When a man is gloomy, everything seems to go
wrong; when he is cheerful, everything seems right!*

—Proverbs 15:15

We all know that gloom brings doom, but we still seem to concentrate on the negative. How many times have you said, "If only"?

- If only…I didn't have this illness.

- If only…I could win the lottery.

- If only…I had a better job.

- If only…my husband made more money.

- If only…my husband was a Christian.

- If only…my son wouldn't run around with that person.

- If only…my parents were still alive.

- If only…if only…if only.

This negative list could go on and on endlessly. The "if onlys" of our lives prevent us from being the person God wants us to be. It's a contagious disease. This type of self-pity is never ending. We get caught in a mind-set that prevents us from turning our lives around.

Your friends won't stick around if all they hear is "If only." Your conversation drains the life from those around you. "If only" causes you to be friendless—so stop it. Instead of "If only," try, "I can!"

Prayer: *Father God, I know you don't want to hear my "If onlys." Help me to be upbeat and bury my negative attitudes. Amen.*

Action: Learn to say, "I can!"

Reflections:

Always Be

*Always be joyful. Always keep on praying.
No matter what happens, always
be thankful, for this is God's will
for you who belong to Christ Jesus.*

—1 THESSALONIANS 5:16-18

If the Bible says it, I believe it. That's a good slogan to live by—as long as we go beyond just believing with our minds and begin to obey with our lives. The Bible means what it says, and that's important to keep in mind.

Today's scripture tells us to *always* be joyful, *always* keep praying, *always* be thankful. Most of us manage to be joyful, to pray, to be thankful sometimes. But always? That's tough—but when God says *always,* He means always! For God's people joy, prayer, and thanksgiving are to be constants. We are supposed to stay simple and pure before the Lord and live out these three attributes of the Christian life consistently. When we do, we not only live in the full flow of God's blessing, but we reflect those blessings to the world around us. Remember, you might be the only Bible some will ever read.

We can't do it without God's help, of course. But that's the heart of the Good News: He's always with us.

Prayer: *Father God, flowers, colors, textures, rain, sunshine, water, soil; You are the wonderful Creator. Produce Your love and goodness in me. Amen.*

Action: Make joy, prayer, and thanksgiving a part of your daily walk.

Reflections:

The Starfish

There was a young man walking down a deserted beach just before dawn. In the distance, he saw a frail old man.

As he approached the old man, he saw him picking up stranded starfish and throwing them back into the sea.

The young man gazed in wonder as the old man again and again threw the small starfish from the sand to the water.

He asked, "Old man, why do you spend so much energy doing what seems to be a waste of time?"

The old man explained that the stranded starfish would die if left in the morning sun.

"But there must be thousands of starfish!" exclaimed the young man. "How can you make any difference?"

The old man looked at the small starfish in his hand, and as he threw it to the safety of the sea, he said, "It makes a difference to this one!"

—ATTRIBUTED TO LOREN EISELEY

It Is Well with My Soul

Yet day by day the Lord also pours out
his steadfast love upon me, and through the night
I sing his songs and pray to God who gives me life.

—PSALM 42:8

oratio G. Spafford wrote a beautiful song to console himself after losing his four daughters when their boat sank as they were traveling to Europe. Upon crossing the approximate spot of the ocean where the boat went down, he wrote these beautiful words to this Christian classic.

> When peace, like a river, attendeth my way,
> When sorrows like sea billows roll;
> Whatever my lot, Thou has taught me to say,
> It is well, it is well, with my soul.
>
> My sin, oh the bliss of this glorious thought!
> My sin, not in part but the whole,
> Is nailed to the cross, and I bear it no more;
> Praise the Lord, praise the Lord, O my soul!
>
> And, Lord, haste the day when my faith shall be sight,
> The clouds be rolled back as a scroll;
> The trump shall resound, and the Lord shall descend,
> Even so, it is well with my soul.

Oh, if we could all sing praises to God after such a tragedy—"It is well with my soul." Here was a man who was able to see the big picture of life. He had a confidence far beyond most of our comprehension. A model for all of us.

Prayer: Father God, I truly want to sing, "It is well with my soul, it is well with my soul." Amen.

Action: In your prayer time, give God your situation and say, "It is well with my soul."

Reflections:

They Are Watching

*So take a new grip with your tired hands,
stand firm on your shaky legs, and mark out
a straight smooth path for your feet so that those
who follow you, though weak and lame,
will not fall and hurt themselves, but become strong.*

—HEBREWS 12:12-13

Illness often changes our appearance. I guess being bald is common to those patients who have had heavy dosages of chemotherapy. As my hair started to fall out in the shower and on my pillowcase, I wondered, *How can I turn this lemon into lemonade?* I decided to have a "haircut party" with my family.

As we gathered that day on the patio, my son, Brad, brought his razor that he uses on the boys for their summer butch haircuts, and he gave me a buzz cut. The children and grandchildren were all gathered around to observe and to take a few historic pictures. I looked so cute that all the men and boys decided they wanted a buzz cut so they could be just like Grammy. This was one of my fond memories of a bad occasion. Everyone was watching to see how I would react. My reaction set the tone for them—I modeled joy for them in a difficult situation. They were watching me!

Prayer: Father God, allow me to see the bright side of a
dark situation. Amen.

Action: Make lemonade out of your lemon.

Reflections:

Good to Be Alone

❧

For the Lord God...says: Only in returning to me
and waiting for me will you be saved;
in quietness and confidence is your strength.

—ISAIAH 30:15

One of the great virtues of the Christian life is learning how to appreciate solitude. As our society gets more technologically advanced, it will become more difficult to be alone. You can't go to a movie anymore without being shaken out of your seat by the loud blasting of special effects. Our music has become so loud that it hurts our ears.

Many times, God's most meaningful touches on our lives come when we are all alone. That is one good thing about illness—it gives us an opportunity to be alone. I have been able to revisit some of the big issues of life while I've laid in my bed. God has provided this sweet time—just between Him and me. Don't wait for illness to occur; schedule time to be alone with God. Take time to go for a long walk in the mountains, in the woods, or by the beach just to be alone with God. Schedule a time just as you would a business appointment. Some of my most creative times happen when I'm alone with God.

Prayer: Father God, our quiet times alone together are some of my most precious times. I cherish my time with You. Amen.

Action: Plan a quiet time with God.

Reflections:

He Hears My Sighs

*Lord, you know how I long for
my health once more.
You hear my every sigh.*

—Psalm 38:9-10

Sometimes in the night my heart lets out a sigh, and my Bob inquires if I am okay. I'm often unaware that a sigh had been uttered. I assure Bob that I am okay, that my soul was just talking to God.

Perhaps my sigh is saying, *Lord, in my sickness and distress, my whole life is open before You. I've hidden nothing from You. You even hear my sighs. At times, my words don't seem adequate; all that are left are the groans of my soul. I look forward to what You will reveal next. Your plan is my plan.*

As my journey seems to be going in the direction of recovery and remission I thank my God every day for how He is restoring my health to where it was. I'm not sure that I will ever be 100 percent back to normal, but I am joyful for where I am.

I have a God who is concerned for my every need. He longs to restore me to good health. One of the big mysteries of life is why He has given restored health to me and not to others. He is the Potter of life—I just have to trust Him in life and death.

Prayer: Father God, satisfy my soul with Your joy, love, and forgiveness. Everything else is just window dressing. Amen.

Action: Don't stop your sighs—they are meant for God to hear.

Reflections:

God hath not promised
Skies always blue,
Flower-strewn pathways
All our lives through.
God hath not promised
Sun without rain,
Joy without sorrow,
Peace without pain.

But God hath promised
Strength for the day,
Rest for the laborer,
Light for the way.
Grace for the trials,
Help from above,
Unfailing sympathy,
Undying love.

—ANNIE FLINT

Like a Deer

The Lord God is my Strength,
and he will give me the speed of a deer
and bring me safely over the mountains.

—HABAKKUK 3:19

eer are such beautiful animals. When I was a child, Walt Disney made Bambi come alive. My heart has always been tender to the deer family. They are so agile and run at such speed, even on mountainous terrain.

I am blessed just to know that God makes my feet as swift as a deer's and that He enables me to travel safely over higher plains. When we vacation in the mountains, we love to see the deer on the ridges across the valley. They run with such swiftness, and their lungs are conditioned to race to the highest peak. That's the way I want my life to function. I want to run swiftly toward the mark and respond to the highest calling. His strength is sufficient for me.

Just to know that my God is all-knowing and that He has power over everything gives me solace. This truth gives me such assurance that He is capable of doing what He says.

Prayer: Father God, what would I do without Your grace? Humble me so that I might receive more of Your grace. Break me so that I can be made whole. Amen.

Action: Trust God more!

Reflections:

The Four "With Alls"

*And you shall love the Lord your God
with all your heart, and with all your soul,
and with all your mind, and with all your strength.*

—MARK 12:30 NASB

Since the 1960s our culture has encouraged each of us to "do your own thing." You know the mottos: "I know what's best for me," "Don't tell me what to do," "If it feels good, do it." In the wake of those values, we've seen an increasing lack of accountability in each succeeding generation.

In contrast, one noted Christian said, "The rule that governs me is this: Anything that dims my vision of Christ or my prayer life, or makes Christian work difficult, is wrong for me, and I must, as a Christian, turn away from it."

Which motto do you want to live by? The first value will be broadcast loud and clear repeatedly throughout our lives. If we are going to learn anything different—if we are to live with godly values and be willing to assume responsibility for our actions—it's up to us to make it happen. You don't learn these things by accident.

Search your heart today and see if you are accepting responsibilities readily, admitting your mistakes easily, and serving God with all your being.

How are you to love God?

- ❧ with all your heart
- ❧ with all your soul
- ❧ with all your mind
- ❧ with all your strength

Prayer: *Father God, give me the will and power to love You with these "with alls." I want to continue to have the passion to love You this way every day. Amen.*

Action: Make good choices that guide you to love God.

Reflections:

God Preserves Your Tears

*You have seen me tossing and turning through
the night. You have collected all my tears
and preserved them in your bottle!
You have recorded every one in your book.*

—PSALM 56:8

David was amazed that God was attentive to every detail of his life—even down to the tears he shed. It truly is amazing to think that our God is so intimately concerned for us that He notices our tears and saves them in His bottle.

During my journey, I have shed many tears—some of joy and some of pain. Even minor tears are huge to the one who cries. God uses these times to cleanse us. Don't be afraid to cry. It is very therapeutic for the soul. Our culture doesn't look favorably on those who cry, but don't let that hold you back. God says that He preserves each and every one of our tears.

We must hope to be mowers,
And to gather the ripe gold ears,
Unless we have first been sowers
And watered the furrows with tears.

It is not just as we take it,
This mystical world of ours,
Life's field will yield as we make it
A harvest of thorns or of flowers.

—JOHANN WOLFGANG VON GOETHE

Prayer: *Father God, You are with me every time I shed a tear for whatever reason. I'm also confident that You are crying when I cry. We both know that there will be a shout of joy in the morning. Amen.*

Action: Know that when you cry, God cries along with you.

Reflections:

If It's God's Will

What you ought to say is, "If the Lord wants us to,
we shall live and do this or that."

—James 4:15

One thing I've learned through this illness is that life is very uncertain. We can say we will do this or that, but we can't know for sure it will happen. I've had to change so many plans because of illness, change of mind, change of priorities, or because God simply intervenes and rearranges everything.

That doesn't mean I've become negative or that I've lost hope along the way. It means I've begun to realize that God has a master plan behind all of His mysteries. Only God knows what the future holds.

Lately, I have been studying the Lord's Prayer (Matthew 6:9-13 KJV), "Our Father which art in heaven, Hallowed be Thy name. Thy Kingdom come, Thy will be done." Yes, Thy will be done. After all these years, I am still learning to accept and praise God for letting "Thy will be done" in my life.

We all have different opportunities and challenges. But as believers in Christ, we can rest assured that He has the very best in mind for our lives. We are to...

- Make God first in our lives—make Him number one.

- Realize that God has a plan for our lives.

⚘ Remember that whatever comes—comes from God. We are nothing without Him.

⚘ Decide that all we have and all we do, we will do it to the glory of God.

Prayer: *Father God, light my path so I will not stumble. Guide me into this wisdom, "Thy will be done." Amen.*

Action: Realize that God has a plan for your life.

Reflections:

Redemption of Time

❦

I will make up to you for the years
that the swarming locust has eaten...
you will have plenty to eat and be satisfied
and praise the name of the LORD your God.

—JOEL 2:25-26 NASB

In America, rural farmers have been devastated by the invasion of swarming locusts. Farmers have had to move hundreds of miles and, on occasion, have had to find a new line of work because the locusts destroyed their way of life.

But God is a God of restoration! Even when the devastation to a human being is like the work of a swarm of locusts on a promising crop—even then, God promises to completely restore everything that has been destroyed.

Have the locusts eaten anything of yours? Your health, a job, a reputation, a husband, a friend? We all have had losses due to locusts in our lives. Perhaps you have already seen God's restoration and are rejoicing. But you may still be looking out over the fields that were once full and rich with bounty—now destroyed.

Look up! Your fields can be restored. The Savior's promise for Israel can also be claimed for your life. Yes, you can even praise God for the locusts of the past. Their devastation is simply a pathway for God to move—and when God moves to restore, He does an awesome job. God renews our past by renewing our present. He gives us new peace, new joy, new goals, new dreams, and new love. What God has promised, He will do!

Prayer: Father God, please restore my health. The locusts have stripped me and I need to be encouraged. Amen.

Action: Let God restore whatever the locusts have damaged in your life.

Reflections:

God Gives Comfort

*Thy rod and Thy staff,
they comfort me.*

—PSALM 23:4 KJV

The shepherd protects his sheep with his rod or club (used to fight off wild beasts), and he guides straying sheep with his staff or crook.

The great English preacher Charles Spurgeon reflected on this great comfort:

> Give me the comforts of God, and I can well bear the taunts of men. Let me lay my head on the bosom of Jesus, and I fear not the distraction of care and trouble. If my God will give the light of His smile, and glance His benediction, it is enough. Come on foes, persecutors...the Lord God is my sun and shield. I carry a sun within; blow, wind of the frozen north, I have a fire of living coal within; yea death slay me, but I have another life—a life in the light of God's countenance.

Here was a man who knew that Jesus was all he needed. He was secure in his faith and realized that his comfort came from the rod and staff of his Shepherd—Jesus Christ.

Take a look at your daily newspaper or TV news and you will realize that we face ongoing problems of violence, life-threatening disease, and political uncertainty every day.

The challenge of the Christian is to live *in* the world but *not* by its standards. To live by the world's standards is to have the world's strength in the day of trouble. To live by God's grace is to have God's strength in the day of trouble.

Prayer: *Father God, through the years You have protected and guided me with Your rod and staff. You have upheld me in times of weakness. I appreciate the strength and comfort You have given me. Amen.*

Action: Come alongside one who needs your strength.

Reflections:

□ □ □

Be Silent

❦

Stand silent! Know that I am God!

—Psalm 46:10

"Stand silent! Know that I am God!" our heavenly Father urges. Easier said than done, right? So many women share with me, "I'm just dying for a little peace and quiet—a chance to relax and think and pray. Somehow I just can't seem to find that for my life."

Stillness and silence are not words many of us even use anymore, let alone experience. Women today, perhaps more than at any other time in history, desperately need the spirit of stillness. I can truly say one of the pluses of my illness has been the opportunity to experience silence and stillness. Hour after hour I have had to sit in a doctor's office or hospital, waiting for something. Almost every day for five years I have had to lay down for a nap. These are precious times, and I wouldn't trade them for anything. Too bad that it took an illness to teach me to clear my calendar in order to find these precious times of quietness.

Do whatever is necessary to nurture the spirit of silence in your life. Don't let the enemy wear you down and steal your balance and perspective. Regular time for silence is as important and necessary as sleep, exercise, and nutritious food. The door to silence and stillness is there waiting for any of us to open and go through—it won't open by itself.

Prayer: Father God, let me choose to be still. Give me the
            courage to turn off all the noise in my life so I can
            spend time alone with You. Amen.

Action: Block out at least 15 minutes on your daily
            calendar to have silence and stillness.

Reflections:

Don't Forsake Me

❧

And now that I am old and gray, don't forsake me.
Give me time to tell this new generation
(and their children too) about all your mighty miracles.

—Psalm 71:18

As I get older, I think more and more about what comes next. I know that something must follow after this life is over because I can't grasp the alternatives. I can't imagine that through all eternity I'll never see anyone I love again, that my whole awareness will just be obliterated. I don't believe that we're only bodies passing through.

There is a season of life that challenges our belief of the hereafter. What happens when we die? The psalmist pleads for God not to forsake him until he declares the power of God to the next generation. Wow! What a great prayer! I guess that's why I do what I do. I want to tell everyone, starting with my immediate family and branching out to others, about the power and the might of God.

One of my favorite passages of Scripture gives me a vision of how I can touch the next generation. It's found in Titus 2:3-6 (NIV): "Likewise, teach the older women to be reverent in the way they live, not to be slanderous or addicted to much wine, but to teach what is good. Then they can train the younger women to love their husbands and children, to be self-controlled and pure." If only we could grasp the vastness of these words. Don't wait until you are old and gray haired. Begin today!

Prayer: *Father God, I need You. Take control of the throne of my life. Make me the kind of person You want me to be. Amen.*

Action: Decide to be a woman (at whatever age) of God. Share with those you love about the Gospel.

Reflections:

Attitude

A wise man is strong,
and a man of knowledge increases power.

—PROVERBS 24:5 NASB

Grandchildren are so much fun. My five give me such great examples and illustrations for my writing and speaking. If I listen and watch, I can observe and hear all about life. I have one grandson, Chad, who is 17 years old. He is either up or down—no halfway point for him. His highs are as extreme as his lows. Attitude is his saint or his demon. Over the years his biggest enemy is his attitude. For his birthday a few years ago, we gave him a coffee cup with the word "attitude" printed in large letters. He placed it as a reminder on a shelf, over his bed, so that each day upon waking he spots this cup. The printed letters are a reminder that he can choose the proper attitude for the day.

I believe that this is the single most significant decision that one can make on a day-to-day basis. The attitude I choose either keeps me on a positive path or hinders my progress. When my attitudes are proper, nothing can stop me from accomplishing my dreams. Even when we are in a deep valley—no illness is too great for us. Our attitude is up to us.

Prayer: Father God, encourage me to have a good attitude
each day. Let no barrier come into my life today
that gives me a bad attitude. Amen.

Action: Choose to have a good attitude today.

Reflections:

Never Give Up

❧

We never give up. Though our bodies are dying,
our inner strength in the Lord is growing every day.

—2 CORINTHIANS 4:16

I f you have financial troubles, setbacks...it's not the end.

If you have been lied to and deceived...it's not the end.

If you have lost your job...it's not the end.

If you have lost your home...it's not the end.

If something has been stolen from you or if you have been robbed of your inheritance...it's not the end.

If you have a child who is ensnared in sin, entangled in a web of wrong relationships, failing according to life's report card, or refusing to communicate with you...it's not the end.

If your mate has walked away, chosen someone else instead of you...it's not the end.

If you have just lost a loved one to death—sudden death, expected or unexpected—it's not the end. Even if your loved one committed suicide...it's not the end.

If you are incarcerated for a crime—it's not the end.

If you are losing your hearing or your sight—it's not the end.

If you are in the depths of depression, if you are battling depression or a chemical imbalance that has thrown all your emotions and even your way of doing things out of kilter...it's not the end.

If you have learned that you have a terminal disease, a crippling disease, a wasting disease...it's not the end.

If you have stepped onto the threshold of death...it's not the end.

I can tell you all this with the utmost of confidence and know that what I am telling you is truth.

It may seem like the end...

You may wish it were the end...

But it is not the end because God is God and the end has not yet come.

—FROM A KAY ARTHUR NEWSLETTER*

 Prayer: *Father God, thank You again for assuring me that this isn't the end, for the end will be an "eternal weight of glory" far beyond all comparison. I trust You for perfecting what's taking place in my life. Amen.*

Action: In your journal, list several of your temporary afflictions. Beside each one, write, "This is producing an eternal weight of glory for me."

Reflections:

---

* Used by permission.

Sing a New Song

❧

He has given me a new song to sing,
of praises to our God. Now many will hear
of the glorious things he did for me,
and stand in awe before the Lord,
and put their trust in him.

—PSALM 40:3

What would our life be without joy? Without joy, we can do nothing. We would be like a harsh, out-of-tune violin. Life without joy is like a dislocated bone; it doesn't function properly. We can do nothing well without joy.

Our doctors and nurses look forward to Bob and my visits to their office—they know we will enliven them with joy. So many patients come there as victims rather than victors. I have chosen to reflect the love of Jesus instead.

God will put a new song in our hearts and a hymn of praise on our lips. When we confess our sins to God with an open heart, He is faithful and just to forgive our sins and cleanse us from all unrighteousness. With this emptying of our old self, He will give us a new song. He has a new song just for *you*.

As a family, we can take this promise and extend our joy and song into laughter. A good laugh is healthy to the body—develop a habit of laughter.

Prayer: Father God, I need a new song in my heart. The enemy of my soul is formidable. But I know that your Word is true: Greater is He that is in me than he that is in the world. Amen.

Action: Look for something today that will help you laugh.

Reflections:

Don't Be Afraid

Don't be troubled or afraid.

—JOHN 14:27

One of your first reactions when a doctor tells you that you have a very serious illness is fear. I can vividly remember the first examination I had with Dr. Barth, my oncologist. As our family gathered around the walls of the conference room, he announced I had a very advanced stage of lymphoma and he needed to start me on chemotherapy. My heart sank as our children broke into tears. They were saddened to hear the bad news.

Humanly speaking, I was *afraid*. It took some time for me to realize that I was starting a journey that I had never been on before. None of my family or close friends had been there either. I felt so alone—no voice of experience to call on.

As days passed and the news finally sank in, I began to find new comfort and strength in Scripture. God's promises gave me courage I had never known before and strength that was pent up inside me. Looking back over these last five years, I can truly say, *Don't be afraid!* I've learned to trust God more—you can, too.

Prayer: Father God, thank You for the courage to fight
              any fear. As I take one day at a time, You give me
              unbelievable courage to face each day. Amen.

Action: Read some Psalms.

Reflections:

God has not promised there will always
be sunshine in our lives.
but He has promised that His light
will always be there for us.

—EMILIE BARNES

More than Words

❦

For I am convinced that nothing can ever
separate us from his love. Death can't, and life can't.
The angels won't, and all the powers
of hell itself cannot keep God's love away.

—ROMANS 8:38

Words, words, words! Sometimes that's what the Bible seems to me. Sometimes it seems confusing or hard to understand.

Sometimes—especially when life was going well—I would read through whole passages without any sense of what the words really meant.

But during the tough times, the times when my life began to crumble, I found that the words of Scripture really came to life. Passages that I had previously read and memorized were leaping to my mind and helping me cope with my situation. The Word suddenly took on a new depth of meaning.

The familiar words of Romans 8 were a wonderful comfort. They remind me that the Lord is with me in my pain, but He also is greater than my current illness. He is larger than my pain, larger than any fear I may have, and larger even than death. I have often needed that assurance, and been unsure of my own strength.

Nothing can separate me from God's love—and that's more than just words! That's rock-solid, dependable, life-giving truth.

Prayer: Lord God Almighty, You are perfect in power and love. Amen.

Action: Believe that nothing can separate you from God's love.

Reflections:

He Guides All the Way

*Even when walking through the dark valley of death
I will not be afraid, for you are close beside me,
guarding, guiding all the way.*

—PSALM 23:4

In the past five years, I have walked many miles through the dark valley of pain and the fear of death. But even in my darkest hour, God has been my comfort. Without His loving arms wrapped around me, I truly could not have survived!

God has sent His loving servants to hold my hands, rub my feet, bring bouquets of flowers and family photos to brighten my room, even clean my house! While in Seattle, we had a dear friend who picked up our dirty laundry each week. In a few days she returned it all folded and ironed—this was a special gift of love. I trust you have friends who treat you the same way.

God has also given me encouraging words through Scripture. And when I gave in to self-pity, He gently admonished me, disciplined me and led me back toward the comforting awareness of His presence. This was during my lowest point. With this kind of love, I know that I'm loved and that I will be taken care of in the future. Thanks be to God, for He has been closer than a sister.

Prayer: Father God, Your Word says that I'm always to be
            thankful; I am so thankful for all Your support
            during this time of trial. Amen.

Action: Do unto others as you would have others do
            unto you!

Reflections:

□ □ □

He Has Overcome

🌺

*I have learned the secret of contentment
in every situation...for I can do everything
God asks me to with the help of Christ
who gives me the strength and power.*

—PHILIPPIANS 4:12-13

Why are so many people surprised when life is difficult? In America we think that everything should be perfect: our marriage, our children, our government, our health, etc. Jesus told us life would be difficult and troublesome. However, so many think they're entitled to a trouble-free life—nothing but happiness, fun, and financial success. Then, when trouble inevitably comes, they're devastated. I have learned to expect the problems and let them teach me something...such as what's really important in life.

Through this long bout of discomfort, I've had a lot more time to ponder just that. The little things that are free have gone up in my value system—a baby's hug, a sea breeze, a call from a friend. Supposedly big issues, such as money and prestige, have gone way down the list.

Best of all, I'm learning it's possible to feel content and peaceful even while bad things are happening—because I know it's all temporary. I can expect pain and trouble because that's part of living in the world, but I can trust God's promise that He'll carry me through it all.

Prayer: Father God, just as You told the waves of Galilee,
             "Quiet, be still," calm the waves in my soul. Still
             the waters; come to me and bring me peace. Amen.

Action: List three eternal blessings God has given
             you. Ponder each one and let it help you be
             contented.

Reflections:

Share Your Cup

❦

God has given each of you some special abilities;
be sure to use them to help each other,
passing on to others God's many kinds of blessings.

—1 PETER 4:10

When the Lord fills our cup, He intends to pour it out. He encourages us to fill the cups of others the best way we know how. And when we do, the sweetness of His love and peace flows from cup to cup. I would never have guessed when I was a young wife many years ago that one day I would write books and conduct large seminars telling women how to get organized, how to care for a home, how to love their families, and to live as a woman of God. You see, I only had a high-school education and didn't feel adequate to tell anyone what to do!

Little by little, other women started to recognize my gifts for organization and speaking. They began to affirm my worthiness, and some even invited me to share what I knew with other women's groups. Over the years, as I have made use of my gifts to administer God's grace to others, I've felt His grace overflow in my own life as well.

Don't let this time in your life go unchallenged. Even in your season of despair, reach up and grab on to helping others with the gift God has given you.

Prayer: Father God, my prayer is that each person will discover and use the gifts You have given her to help someone along the way. Amen.

Action: Use the gifts God has given you.

Reflections:

Patience—Hurry up!

🍂

Cross-examine me, O Lord, and see that this is so;
test my motives and affections too.
For I have taken your lovingkindness
and your truth as my ideals.

—PSALM 26:2-3

Yes, Lord, I prayed to learn patience, but did You have to take me so literally? Was it really necessary for me to go through all the pain, blood transfusing, CAT scans, and other inconveniences that go with cancer treatment? I was ready for some little pop quizzes; I didn't really want the final exam!

This illness has indeed been the hardest test of my life. At times, I have wondered if I'm up to it. Yet even in the midst of all the difficulties, I can see a little of what God is doing in my life. For one thing, this ordeal has forced me to examine my inmost heart—what I truly believe, what I am about, what my priorities are, and what I want to stand for. And my "motives and affections" have withstood the examination! During my time of testing, I have confirmed that God's ideals really are my ideals, and that I want to walk in faithfulness to Him.

Now, if only I could get the patience a little faster...

Prayer: Father God, I have learned so much about patience. After a lot of time, trials, and suffering, I think I'm learning how to wait. Amen.

Action: Today, be patient with something that would normally irritate you.

Reflections:

Day by Day

Your heavenly Father knows your needs.
He will always give you all you need
from day to day.

—LUKE 12:30-31

As of today, I have lived through 23,399 days, and I have found this promise in Luke to be true in my life everyday. I've had my ups and downs, but God has always provided for my needs. As a little girl with an alcoholic, sometimes violent father, I was protected. As a teenager living with my single-parent mom in the little apartment behind our dress store, I never went hungry or unclothed. Money was often tight, but I can't remember not having the necessities of life. We had a roof over our head and a loving family.

As newlyweds in a tiny apartment, Bob and I often struggled to make ends meet, but there was always enough from day to day.

Now, during my adult years, the Lord has graciously blessed me beyond all my expectations—materially and spiritually. God is truly the provider of all good things. Bob shared with me recently that this was the best time in our lives—what a miracle statement!

Prayer: *Father God, I appreciate all that you do for us. You have orchestrated each day of my life. Thank you for providing my daily provisions. Amen.*

Action: Count your blessings; name them one by one.

Reflections:

Come Quick

Don't hide from me, for I am in deep trouble.
Quick! Come and save me.
Come, Lord, and rescue me.

—Psalm 69:17-18

We want God to work everything out right now. Not tomorrow, but now—and hurry up. When I became sick, I just wanted to get well—fast. *Just give me the chemo and radiation, and in a few months I will be back to my usual routine of life.* I didn't mind being sick for a little while, because I knew the doctors and pharmacists had enough skills to solve my problems. Unlike Humpty Dumpty when he fell off the wall, I just wanted to be put back together again.

The truth of the matter is, God will rescue me—but in His time, not at my hurried pace. I certainly appreciate God's loving patience with me. I want to be known as a person of *being*—not just *doing*. I often plead to God to keep me humble. Well, He has done that, for a good five years. I appreciate what God has done in my life. He has put a strong desire in my soul to spend time every day with Him. I ask, "Let time stand still and let me forget all about my schedule." I want to keep my focus on Him.

Prayer: *Father God, Thank You for slowing me down. Now I don't run the red lights of life. I really like my new pace. Amen.*

Action: Get off the merry-go-round before it throws you off.

Reflections:

Notice the Shadows of His Wings

How precious is your constant love, O God!
All humanity takes refuge
in the shadow of your wings.

—PSALM 36:7

As a young girl, I loved to look down at the sidewalk on a bright sunny day and see the shadows of the clouds and planes as they flew overhead. Living in a warm climate, I appreciated the big clouds because they blocked out the sun's hot rays and gave some relief from the heat. I can only imagine what kind of shadow God's wings would cast.

I know it would be much larger than that of a sparrow, even larger than an American bald eagle or even a California condor. I can just feel His cool shade. I'm so glad I can relax in the cool shadow of His mighty wings.

My cancer journey has given me a wonderful opportunity to do things in a new way. I've been able to truly be still and know that He is God. I was so caught up in such a hectic pace that I didn't take the time to look up toward heaven and see His big puffy clouds or look down and pay attention to the shadows on the sidewalk. Now I simply make the time.

Prayer: *Father God, thank You for reminding me to take time and revel in the shadows of Your wings. Amen.*

Action: Take time to notice the clouds and shadows in your life.

Reflections:

Keep Your Powder Dry

We felt we were doomed to die and saw
how powerless we were to help ourselves;
but that was good, for then we put everything
into the hands of God, who alone could save us.

—2 CORINTHIANS 1:9

Revolutionary War soldiers had a famous motto: "Trust in God, but keep your powder dry!" We are to trust God in everything, but we must use common sense. We must do all we can to fight disease. Not only do we trust our Lord in all aspects, but as patients we must do all we can to find out how to conquer our illness. We can "keep our powder dry" by:

- Taking responsibility to find out about your illness.

- Getting a second opinion if necessary.

- Searching the Internet.

- Talking to those who have a similar illness.

- Trusting your medical team or getting a new team.

- Asking a lot of questions from those providing medical care.

- Praying and asking others to pray for you.

- Being a good patient—doing what you are told to do.

- Being positive and upbeat.
- Telling your family the good stuff and telling God the bad.

Prayer: *Father God, we know that You are the Healer of all illnesses. Help me to find out all I can so I can have the proper attitude toward healing.*

Action: Keep your powder dry.

Reflections:

Don't Fear Your Limits

❧

But you are merciful and gentle, Lord,
slow in getting angry,
full of constant lovingkindness and of truth.

—PSALM 86:15

We humans tend to put great expectations on ourselves. We think if we don't meet a certain performance level, God will judge us. We tend to grade ourselves with negative points if we do this or if we don't do that.

God understands our limits. He knows our struggles before they even transpire. God knows how much pressure and stress we can endure. And with this awareness, He knows how much grace, mercy, and strength will be required. Since we are all uniquely made in His image, He knows us very well.

During various trials of life, we need to be aware that He does care for us. Remember, nothing happens to us that isn't first approved by our heavenly Father. He is molding and making us in His way. You can handle everything that comes your way.

Prayer: Father God, thank You for screening out all those
              things that I can't handle. Give me the power to
              endure every situation that comes my way. Amen.

Action: Rest assured you can overcome with God's
              grace.

Reflections:

Even the most tragic happenings
will be turned into good
for those who love the Lord
and are His Children. Our spiritual rearing
is moved along by difficulties we face
and the mountains we climb.

—DOROTHY KELLEY PATTERSON

□ □ □

This Sickness Is Not unto Death

*This sickness is not unto death,
but for the glory of God,
that the Son of God may be glorified by it.*

—JOHN 11:4 NASB

azarus, the brother of Mary, had become very ill and was near death. Being good friends of Jesus, Lazarus' family had sent word for Him to come and heal Lazarus. But Jesus did not drop everything to go; instead, He tarried two more days where He was. As a result, Lazarus died. His family, confused and hurt by Jesus' apparent lack of concern, wrapped Lazarus in burial clothes, placed him in a tomb, and closed the entrance with a large stone.

When Jesus did arrive, Lazarus had been dead for four days, and his body had begun to decay. Yet Jesus said, "Lazarus, come forth!" The people knew he was dead, but they believed he would arise again the last day because Jesus said, "I am the resurrection and the life; he who believes in Me shall live even if he dies, and everyone who lives and believes in Me shall never die. Do you believe this?"

This is where I was tested. *Did I truly believe that I would never die?* I came to accept death as part of life. When I realized this, I was truly free to live.

125

I could appreciate the family's anger at Jesus for not coming as expected. I, too, was disappointed when Jesus didn't answer my prayers immediately. *Why, God? You need to be with me—please don't tarry where You are. Please come now.*

Prayer: Father God, I've called out to You for healing, and I've been disappointed when You haven't done what I've expected. Let me be patient with Your calendar. I know You don't set Your clock by my watch. Even unto death, I believe that You have planned my coming in and my going out. Amen.

Action: Know that God hears your every prayer and that you can accept His will for your life.

Reflections:

Choose to
Be Grateful

❦

Go through his open gates with great thanksgiving;
enter his courts with praise.
Give thanks to him and bless his name.

—PSALM 100:4

f only I could take a shopping cart to Target or Wal-Mart and shop until I had all the stuff I wanted—then I would be happy! Have you echoed that thought before? I have a very close friend who often verbalized, "If only I could have a bigger house, a bigger car, a bigger ring...then I would be happy." After 25 years, she is still looking for happiness in possessions. She's looking for happiness in all the wrong places.

The Scriptures are quite clear that a thoughtful heart is a happy heart. To have complete happiness, we must enter into the Lord's presence with thanksgiving. I have found that when I am appreciative for all I have, my spirit, soul, and body are healthier.

As the years fly by, Bob and I continually discuss how grateful we are to have each other. We count our blessings on a regular basis. Even during an illness, choose to be grateful.

Prayer: Father God, don't let me become wrapped up in
             earthly possessions. I want my happiness to come
             from you. Amen.

Action: Tonight, tell your husband or wife how much
             you appreciate him or her!

Reflections:

No Greater Love

For God so loved the world,
that He gave His only begotten Son,
that whoever believes in Him shall not perish,
but have eternal life.

—JOHN 3:16 NASB

John 3:16 contains the greatest promise in the Scriptures. Without it, all the rest would be meaningless. By sacrificing His Son, God gave us a way to be with Him forever.

I so want to grasp this concept and pledge every day to living out its truth. *Lord, I know that I'm living out eternity now! I don't have to wait until I die to be with You because today is part of eternity. Thank You for Your ultimate gift.*

My sunshine on one cloudy Seattle day was sharing this verse of Scripture with a young man named Marshall. Bob and I had the opportunity to tell him about this great gift one Sunday morning when we met for prayer. He was very sick and had a terrible infection that could not be cured. The day of his passing, Marshall confirmed that he believed the truths of this scripture. We had the pleasure of assuring him and his family that today he would be in paradise with Jesus. What a wonderful moment.

Prayer: Father God, let me rest in Your presence and Your promised guidance. As the Scripture says, "You surround me with songs of deliverance." Amen.

Action: Share John 3:16 with someone today.

Reflections:

Check Your Attitude

❧

A faithful [woman] will abound with blessings.

—PROVERBS 28:20 NASB

on't spend time thinking about what you don't have. Instead, count your blessings and be thankful for the things you do have. Don't wait for the next big positive thing to occur in your life before you get excited. Get excited now. Find happiness where you are. Make the most of what you have.

One way to relieve stress is to stop using your situation to justify your unhappiness. Learn to stop saying, "If only...." Enjoy what you have to the maximum.

The young children who were undergoing chemo and radiation in Seattle were great inspirations to me. They continued to run, jump, and laugh even while dragging their tubes and fanny packs along with them. Children have such a marvelous attitude about their situation. We adults should be more childlike. Even when we aren't feeling well, we need to run, jump, and laugh like children. Many times our blessings are determined by our attitude.

Prayer: *Father God, thanks for sticking with me. Please encourage me to run, jump and laugh. I appreciate all Your blessings. Amen.*

Action: Run, jump, and laugh.

Reflections:

Start Your Day Out Right

But I called upon the Lord in my distress, and he heard me from his Temple.

—2 SAMUEL 22:7

I woke up this morning and smiled
at my new day.
I combed my hair, brushed my teeth,
laid out my fine pressed clothes,
nearly panicked for my glasses
when I found them on my nose.
Ran out of the house, jumped in my car,
and away to work I flew,

Alongside me pulled a maniac
and I just didn't know what to do.
I looked real close, then realized
he must just be some flirt;
I took a closer look and he was saying lady,
your door, your shirt.

Well, Lord, my day has yet to begin
and already I'm a mess,
unorganized and running late,
not to mention my forgetfulness.

A few more hours in my day, Lord,
I think that would get me by,
with the hours I have now, Lord,
the day just seems to fly.

"My child," He said, "I've given you
everything you need,
My plan is perfect, it's My direction
you do not heed.
Start your day in prayer
and soon you'll begin to see,
It's not the hours in your day that count,
it's how you spend your time with me."

—NANCY LING

What an awesome truth. When we don't start out our day in prayer, the world's forces attack us. But when we begin our day with a time of prayer, we come under God's umbrella and are protected from the world's forces. Don't be in a hurry except to rush to the foot of the cross each day.

Prayer: *Father God, help me to set my affections on things above. Help me to seek Your kingdom first. I want my life to reflect Your presence. Slow me down. Amen.*

Action: Start today with a quiet time with the Lord.

Reflections:

Leap Like a Calf

But for you who fear my name,
the Sun of Righteousness will rise
with healing in his wings.
And you will go free, leaping with joy
like calves let out to pasture.

—MALACHI 4:2

I claim this promise for myself—that God is able to heal me of my illness and that He will heal me according to His purposes. One way or another, I believe a miracle of healing is being done in my life, and I thank God He is able to accomplish this.

I know that my God is above all that is in the world and that He owns everything. The cattle on a thousand hills are His, and He knows the number of grains of sand on all the beaches. He has created all the stars, and He knows each of them by their name. He made me and knows me, too. God is an omnipotent helper, and He gives me an abundance of strength. I look forward to the day of my full recovery on this earth.

And I am looking forward to the day when I can leap like a calf being released to pasture. That's going to be some amazing day.

Prayer: Father God, I appreciate the degree of healing You have given me. At times it doesn't seem much, but looking back at the last two years it has been remarkable.

Action: Go out and leap like a calf.

Reflections:

Trust and Obey

❧

But Jesus immediately spoke to them,
reassuring them. "Don't be afraid!" he said.

—MATTHEW 14:27

When the waves of life threaten to engulf us, we can keep our eyes on Him and face the storm with complete trust. "I will trust and not be afraid" (Isaiah 12:2).

Each of us have storms sweep across our horizons. We can be overcome by fear and doubt and begin to sink, or we can be filled with faith and trust and walk triumphantly on the stormy waves. We have the option to put our trust completely in Him and His promises. Fear and trust don't go together. They are like oil and water. If trust is the oil, it will rise to the top; if fear is the oil, then it will rise to the top. Which one is your oil?

James H. Sammis' classic hymn "Trust and Obey" includes this chorus: "Trust and obey, for there's no other way to be happy in Jesus, but to trust and obey."

Prayer: Father God, You have given me an opportunity to take the words of this great hymn and apply it to my life. You have been faithful to Your promise. Amen.

Action: Let trust be the oil of your life.

Reflections:

No More Tears

❧

He will wipe away all tears from their eyes,
and there shall be no more death,
nor sorrow, nor crying, nor pain.
All of that has gone forever.

—REVELATION 21:4

Who else can give us a promise like this one? It's an exciting glimpse of what life in eternity with Him will be like.

Just think of life with no more tears, no more death, no more sorrow, no more crying! No more of the familiar, unavoidable pain of being human. These will all disappear forever. Hard to imagine, isn't it? We live in a fallen and depraved world; as a result, our lives are often dysfunctional. Pain and unhappiness are familiar to all of us, regardless of what our position in life might be. Some have illness, some have money troubles, and some agonize over disrupted relationships.

But those who have followed Christ won't live like that forever—we have God's promise on that. Someday all our pain will be wiped away, never to be experienced again. I look forward with great anticipation to that heavenly event. I hope you are there with me.

Prayer: Father God, shine through me this day. Lord, shine Your righteousness, Your strength, and Your truth to all those around me. Shine, Jesus, shine. Amen.

Action: Just meditate on the idea of "no more..."

Reflections:

Dial-a-Friend

Two can accomplish more than twice as much as one,
for the results can be much better.
If one falls, the other pulls him up;
but if a man falls when he is alone, he's in trouble.

—ECCLESIASTES 4:9-10

ecently I spoke on the phone with a darling couple from Iowa. Bob and I met them in Seattle when Barbara and I were being treated experimentally for cancer. We had a lot in common, as did our caregiving husbands. When they returned home, things got very challenging for Barb. They are now driving an hour each way, three days a week, for her dialysis treatments.

As Barb answered the phone, I could tell her voice was very weak. During our chat we both laughed and giggled. I sensed she needed a prayer of encouragement—so we prayed. My heart was very heavy as I hung up. I will probably never see her again on earth, but we will rejoice when we unite in heaven.

When I was very ill, I had at least five friends who were fighting cancer alongside of me. We were such an encouragement to each other, just visiting a short time—nothing long, but just enough to encourage.

Take the time today to call a friend who may be hurting.

Prayer: *Father God, You have given me some dear friends. I love them and they love me. Thank You for the comfort we give each other. Amen.*

Action: Call someone today who needs a lift.

Reflections:

Say Yes for Tomorrow

Rejoice that your names are recorded in heaven.

—LUKE 10:20 NASB

A few days after Roy Rogers passed away at his home in Apple Valley, California, a local Christian television station ran a tribute to his life. One of the segments had Dale Evans, Roy's wife, singing a song titled, "Say Yes for Tomorrow." This song was dedicated to the memory of Roy's early decision to put his trust in Jesus as his Savior.

While listening to this song, I began to think back over my own life. I said "yes for tomorrow" by saying yes to Jesus. My direction for the future was decided. As I've matured, I've realized many adults have never made this affirmation. What a shame to search all one's life and then, at the end of life, be unsure of what the future might hold.

If you haven't settled what tomorrow will be, take time today to guarantee your destination. Confirm to your family that you will be united together forever in heaven.

Prayer: *Father God, I thank You for providing a way for me to know where my tomorrow will be. Amen.*

Action: If you haven't answered the tomorrow question, today might be the day to settle the most important question in your life.

Reflections:

Stay Focused

And thine ears shall hear a word behind thee, saying,
"This is the way, walk ye in it."

—Isaiah 30:21 kjv

ichelangelo said, "Gazing on beautiful things acts on the soul, which thirsts for heavenly light." When we gaze, we concentrate and focus. When we're ill, we have to conserve our energy and eliminate the unnecessary. The key to finishing those many tasks during your day is focus!

Choose a regular time every day to organize your work. Some women find that a few minutes in the early morning are the best. Others like the comfort of organizing in the evening so they awake with a plan already in place. Whatever you decide, stick with it. Soon it will become a habit.

Develop the ability to focus on the part and not the whole. It will take practice, but it can be done. Divide difficult problems into instant tasks. In other words, clean one shelf or drawer at a time. If the task is too large to do in a day, take two or three days.

I have found a "To Do" list very helpful in keeping me focused. I jot down what needs to be done so I don't forget. It's so much fun to cross the items off when they are completed.

Prayer: Father God, don't let my illness cause me to lose
              focus on what needs to be done. Give me the desire
              and energy to keep on going. Amen.

Action: Focus on the important issues.

Reflections:

☐ ☐ ☐

A New Heart

🍂

I will give you one heart and a new spirit;
I will take from you your hearts of stone
and give you tender hearts of love for God.

—Ezekiel 11:19

The number one killer in America is heart failure. Americans tend to place tremendous stress upon that fist-sized muscle called the *heart*. Some of the stress on our heart is caused by the food we eat, our high-pressure lifestyles, and our lack of physical exercise. Other health problems can stress our hearts as well. And some hearts—such as those with congenital defects—are less able to handle stress.

Spiritually speaking, of course, we are all born with a congenital heart problem—sin. We are all sinners and prone to rebel against God's plan for our lives. The more we continue on our own way, the more hardened and scarred our spiritual hearts can become. But we don't have to live that way. God promises that He will give us a new heart and a new spirit—without needles or anesthesia. He can replace our hardened old heart with a tender, loving one. To take advantage of this wonderful opportunity, all we have to do is surrender our hearts to Him. Why wait?

Prayer: Father God, our confidence is based in Your Word. Your Word is true. Let wisdom reign in my life as I put my trust in You. Amen.

Action: Enjoy your new heart and spirit.

Reflections:

You Are Wonderfully Made

O Lord, I will honor and praise your name,
for you are my God; you do such wonderful things!
You planned them long ago.

—Isaiah 25:1

The psalmist expressed it so beautifully: "For You formed my inward parts; You covered me in my mother's womb. I will praise You, for I am fearfully and wonderfully made (Psalm 139:13 NKJV).

What a blessing to remember what those words mean! Without God, I would not have existed. God planned for me a long time ago, and He had a plan for my life even before I was born—before my mother even thought to name me Emilie Marie. I just pray that I have done what I could to fulfill those plans, so I can stand before Him some day and hear Him say, "Well done, good and faithful servant" (Matthew 25:23 NKJV). Even though you are in the pits now, don't stay down. Keep that inner fire alive. Your fight for life will prolong your energy for overcoming your present conflict. Attitude plays a large part in your fight for recovery and healing. Keep looking upward.

Prayer: *Father God, I know that You have placed the creative ability within me to fulfill your plan. Release Your creativity in me today. May the expressions of my life reflect Your goodness. Amen.*

Action: Know that you are uniquely made. Thank God for creating you.

Reflections:

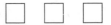

Be Still My Soul

*Wear my yoke—for it fits perfectly—and
let me teach you; for I am gentle and humble,
and you shall find rest for your souls;
for I give you only light burdens.*

—MATTHEW 11:29

We make a big mistake if we forget to calm our spirits and seek the stillness that we need to walk peacefully in this crazy world. The psalmist urged, "Be still, and know that I am God." Easier said than done, right?

Let me urge you today in the strongest possible terms: Do whatever it takes to nurture stillness in your life. Don't let the enemy wear you so thin that you lose your balance and perspective. Regular time for stillness is as important and necessary as sleep, exercise, and nutritious food.

So what's the secret to making time you need for yourself? First, be realistic about what this will look like. You don't have to invest a large block of time. Fifteen minutes here and there can do wonders.

Next, make yourself unavailable to the rest of the world for a few moments each day. Be available to God, to yourself, and then, ultimately, to others. Turn off your cell phone and have all calls go to voice mail.

Prayer: Father God, help me to remember that You came to the world in a simple manger, to a simple man and woman. You came simply to love us. All You ask of me is a simple response.

Action: Be still and available.

Reflections:

Time to Celebrate

*Say "Thank You" to the Lord for being so good,
for always being so loving and kind.*

—PSALM 107:1

Make celebrations a tradition in your family. Why not? Life is for the living—there's always something to celebrate. Just because you are in a difficult fight for renewed health doesn't mean you have to stop celebrating. To the contrary, now is when you really want to celebrate all those important events in life.

Celebrate everything—good days, bad days that are finally over, birthdays, and even nonbirthdays! Get the whole family involved preparing for a dinner celebration. Make it special. Let them make placecards, set the table, help you cook, and create a centerpiece.

Let your celebration sharing extend beyond the family. Several times a year, create a "love basket" filled with food for a needy family. Or try spending part of your holidays helping out at a shelter or mission.

Purchase a "You Are Special" red plate and use it at mealtime to honor someone special. Allow everyone in the family an opportunity to share why the recipient is so special to them.

Don't limit yourself. Look for ways to celebrate life and those you love!

Prayer: Father God, there are many reasons to celebrate
life today. Let me be a helper for those who want to
celebrate but don't know how. Amen.

Action: Go out and celebrate the ordinary.

Reflections:

The Coming of Joy

❧

Though the fig tree does not bud
and there are no grapes on the vines,
though the olive crop fails and the fields
produce no food…yet I will rejoice in the LORD,
I will be joyful in God my Savior.

—HABAKKUK 3:17-18 NIV

*T*rue joy does not come from material possessions, even though they can be wonderful and enjoyable. It does not come from having a healthy family or a successful career, although those can be meaningful and ful-filling. It doesn't come from physical pleasure or delighting the senses. All these things can be good, but eventually they will all be gone. Real joy—the kind that lasts forever—comes from steadfast trust in the Lord.

Through good times and bad times, through sickness and health, through all sorts of ups and downs, we can still express honest joy because we belong to God, because He has ultimate control over what happens to us, and because we can trust Him to make all things work together for our good. The apostle Paul sets the example in Philippians 4:11 when he states, "I have learned how to get along happily whether I have much or little."

Prayer: *Father God, let my joy be complete in You. I have tasted victory and defeat, but Your joy radiates in my heart. May those around me see the joy You give me. Amen.*

Action: Reflect God's joy in your life.

Reflections:

Jesus Loves Me

Only a fool would say to himself, "There is no God."
And why does he say it? Because of his wicked heart,
his dark and evil deeds. His life is corroded with sin.

—PSALM 53:1

have had several people ask me, "How can you believe that God exists?" Really, it isn't hard at all. One, I can look around at all of God's creation and be in awe of the universe, the plants, the waves of the ocean, and above all, the miracle of childbirth. The seasons show me how creative He is in design and color. A world-renowned artist couldn't paint a prettier picture. God's color palette is beyond description.

Second, the simplicity of my faith is found in the childhood chorus that I learned after coming to accept Jesus as my Savior: "Jesus loves me! this I know, For the Bible tells me so..."

All I know about the majesty of God I have found in the Scriptures. "Every knee shall bow...and every tongue shall confess that Jesus Christ is Lord" (Philippians 2:10-11).

I have faith in God and believe that His Son, Jesus, was born of a virgin, lived on this earth for approximately 33 years, was crucified, died, and rose from the grave after three days. God sent the Holy Spirit to be with us until the ultimate return of Jesus for the church, offering us the gift of salvation. Yes, I believe in God.

Prayer: Father God, thank You for loving me—a sinner—
and for redeeming me. Amen.

Action: Know that Jesus loves you.

Reflections:

Smile

🌿

Wisdom lights up a man's face,
softening its hardness.

—ECCLESIASTES 8:1

They say a smile uses fewer face muscles than does a frown. So let's smile more often—it's less work. Wherever I go, a smile is the common denominator for happiness. I have never turned down a smile sent in my direction, nor have I become angry to anyone who smiles back at me. To me, a smile is a blessing one person can give another. It costs the giver very little, and the receiver takes away a beautiful, unexpected gift. You'll never know when your smile is the only smile a person will receive that day.

A smile does take some effort. It requires sensitivity to notice another person and compassion to choose to connect with them, to share a little something from the heart. A smile might not be returned, but it's never wasted. Shared blessings never are.

While I'm sitting in the doctor's office, I've found that a smile breaks the ice between me and another person so we can talk about our situation. Many times I have used this window of encouragement to lift others' spirits. Often they remark as we depart, "Thank you, your words were a real encouragement." It's okay to smile and to talk to strangers.

Prayer: Father God, let a smile light up my face. I have been blessed; may I be a blessing to someone. Amen.

Action: Give a contagious smile to someone today.

Reflections:

Can't Outgive God

*One man gives freely, yet gains even more;
another withholds unduly, but comes to poverty.
A generous man will prosper;
he who refreshes others will himself be refreshed.*

—Proverbs 11:24-25 NIV

have found this to be a basic principle in life: Giving pays tremendous dividends. Most of our riches are in friends, support groups, and those who give encouragement. As we have refreshed others, the Lord has refreshed us through these gifts.

One of our favorite mottos has been, "You can't outgive God." Mark tells us in his Gospel that if we give up worldly possessions for Christ, we shall receive a hundred times now in the present age—houses, brothers, sisters, mothers, children and land (Mark 10:29-30). Wow! What a return of blessings for those who serve the Lord.

I'm so thankful for all that God has given to me. He has abundantly bestowed so much to me and my family.

Prayer: Father God, the principle of giving has been the best thing You have shared with me. My life is so much richer because of what You have taught me. Thank You. Amen.

Action: Give yourself away.

Reflections:

Say "Thank You"

*You have done so much for me, O Lord.
No wonder I am glad! I sing for joy.*

—PSALM 92:4

When we were raising our children, we were careful to teach them good manners, including saying "thank you." When they received a present or a compliment, we couldn't wait for them to say the two magic words before we would blurt out, "What do you say?" With big bright eyes they would meekly answer, "Thank you." We have continued the tradition with our grandchildren.

Saying "thank you" makes everybody feel a little bit more appreciated. When we receive a lot of attention because of our situation in life we must remember our good manners and say "thank you." During the lowest point of my illness, I just didn't have the energy to write or call a "thank you" to my blessed angels who sent cards, flowers, food, etc. However, my Bob spent hours each week sending off thank-you notes or telephone calls.

If you don't have the energy to do this, ask your caregiver to help you. Bob typed up a thank-you note and an update on my illness and had the message printed on attractive paper. Then he mailed them off to dear ones who contributed to my wellness. We saved a lot of time by not personalizing each one.

Prayer: Father God, I give thanks for my mom, who taught me good manners and to say "thank you." Amen.

Action: Say "thank you" to some deserving person today.

Reflections:

The true test of walking in the Spirit
will not be the way we act but the way we react
to the daily frustration of life.

—BEVERLY LAHAYE

One Step at a Time

How do you know what is going to happen tomorrow?
For the length of your lives is uncertain.

—JAMES 4:15

In an old *McGuffey Reader* I found a story about a clock that had been running for a long, long time on a mantelpiece. One day the clock began to think about how many times during the year ahead it would have to tick. It counted up the seconds: 31,536,000 in one year. The old clock just got too tired and thought, *I can't do it.* It stopped right there. When somebody reminded the clock that it didn't have to tick the 31,536,000 seconds all at one time, but rather one by one, it began to run again and everything was all right.

Sometimes, when I get out of bed early in the morning, the day ahead of me looks very long. So many things to do—appointments to keep, blood checks at the doctor's office, a chest X-ray at the hospital, prescriptions to renew, on and on. Some days are 10 to 12 hours long.

To be honest, sometimes I want to forget it all and crawl back into bed. But a small voice inside of me says, "Emilie, you don't have to do it all at once. Just put your feet on the floor and take the first step of the day." Break up the large block into little pieces. A long journey begins with the first step.

Prayer: *Father God, thank You for allowing me to see the whole picture and to realize it doesn't have to be accomplished all at once. Amen.*

Action: Just put your feet on the floor.

Reflections:

Tested with Fire

You have purified us with fire, O Lord,
like silver in a crucible.

—Psalm 66:10

When pain comes into our lives, we are tempted to ask "Why, Lord? Why, Lord, do the righteous suffer?" If ever there was a man who loved and obeyed God, it was Job. Yet his testing was very dramatic and even painful. Today, all we have to do is pick up the newspaper to read of tragedy touching the just and the unjust.

Everyone has experienced some kind of tragedy. If not yet, it will come. How we handle these events when they happen is key. There are many wonderful support groups available to help us process our pain.

Whatever your test today is, please know that others have experienced similar pain. Don't go through the testing alone. Contact your local church or hospital to find out what programs are offered.

Jesus knows and has also experienced our pain. When I think of the pain He suffered on the cross for me, my load seems much lighter. This has given me more courage to fight my battle. He is always with us to help us get through the tough times of life. Trust Him now.

Prayer: Father God, I know from experience that we rarely grow in good times. It's the intense heat that makes us pure. May I be gold and not wood, hay, or stubble. Amen.

Action: Write a letter to God about how you feel.

Reflections:

☐ ☐ ☐

Celebrate His Presence

*Every morning tell him, "Thank you
for your kindness," and every evening
rejoice in all his faithfulness.*

—Psalm 92:2

Your quiet time is not a gift you give God, but a gift that God gives you. Rather than offering Him your "quiet time," simply offer Him yourself.

Get in the habit of saying, "Good morning, Lord" and "Good evening, Lord." This practice will give you joy in the morning and peace at night. Start and end with some time of simply being with God. Wait a minute before bringing Him all your petitions and concerns. First, remember and be thankful for the prayers He has answered in the past. And let all your praying be preceded by praise. We must remember that in the authority of Jesus' name, we can expect answers to our prayers. We can be courageous in our asking and confident in His answers. We have the privilege of celebrating God's presence—for His faithfulness is a promise and a blessing in one.

I never want to take for granted the beginning of a new day or the ending of that day. Each day is precious to me.

Prayer: *Father God, slow me down. I want to be available*
             for the minute conversation, or the gentle hug, or
             the quick smile. Don't let me miss those important
             opportunities to bless those I love. Amen.

Action: Celebrate and give praises in your mornings
             and evenings.

Reflections:

Knowing God's Plan

For I know the plans I have for you, says the Lord.
They are plans for good and not for evil,
to give you a future and a hope.

—JEREMIAH 29:11

s I'm walking through this journey, I often hear people ask why God allows good people to have this illness or that illness, or even allows some to die of their illness. We should all know that all of God's plans are meant for good and that any evil that comes into our lives isn't because of God's doing.

The enemy of my soul wants me to think differently—he wants me to be confused about where this trial comes from. He wants me to question my faith and let doubting thoughts enter my mind:

- ➴ God doesn't care.

- ➴ You've been left in this mess all by yourself.

- ➴ It's unfair.

- ➴ I'm a good person, and this happens to me, while others who aren't godly are doing fine—no problems.

- ➴ What kind of God allows this to happen?

I might pray, *My trial is more than I can bear—please get me out of here!* But God replies, *Emilie, I know the pain of your heart, I have a plan for your life. I know you feel discouraged and downtrodden, but trust Me.*

Many nights as I went to sleep I uttered, *I trust you, Lord; I trust you, Lord.*

Prayer: *Father God, I trust You with my whole being. I know You have a plan for me, one of Your children. Let me trust You more. Amen.*

Action: Trust God more today.

Reflections:

□ □ □

No More Suffering

🍂

These troubles and sufferings of ours are,
after all, quite small and won't last very long.
Yet this short time of distress will result in
God's richest blessing upon us forever and ever!

—2 CORINTHIANS 4:17

Sometimes when I think about my affliction, it seems so big and I have endured so long, I become discouraged. I can hardly believe this illness is actually happening to me. I want to be well and go back to my normal way of life. This is such an inconvenience to my normal routine. Then, the Holy Spirit reassures me not to lose hope, not to be discouraged. Even though my outer self is decaying, this affliction is light and temporary.

The Scriptures tell me that by enduring these earthly troubles I will inherit blessings for eternity. We look forward to a time and place with no more pain and suffering.

Prayer: *Father God, I truly look forward to that day when*
we will be free of pain and suffering. You have
prepared a special place just for me. Thank You.
Amen.

Action: Think about your eternal blessings. What will
they be?

Reflections:

Light Up My Life

You give them drink from your river of delights.
For with you is the fountain of life;
in your light we see light.

—PSALM 36:8-9 NIV

On our patio, we have a wonderful three-tiered fountain that echoes the splashing of water as it falls from one tier to another. The sound of the water is so tranquil. I just love to sit and listen to its soothing sounds. I feel rejuvenated in a very short time.

Quite often I reflect on all the delights God has bestowed on my life. He has given me more than I would have ever thought possible. He has taken an ordinary person and filled her basket full. Even if my quality of life doesn't get any better, I will praise the Lord for being so good to me. At times, I thought I would never be back to this level of recovery.

The Father's light has certainly illuminated my path. I no longer need to walk in darkness.

Prayer: Father God, Your light lights my life. I pray that its reflection will warm those around me and show them just who You are. Amen.

Action: Be a light to someone today.

Reflections:

Give Me Joy

❧

A cheerful heart does good like medicine,
but a broken spirit makes one sick.

—PROVERBS 17:22

Those of us who are sick certainly don't want to take any more pills, injections, transfusions, or bags of liquid. However, I have found the best medicine of all: joy in your heart. But how do you have joy when you are so sick—even having difficulty keeping food and medicine down? During long periods of treatment, keeping anything down is very problematic.

You have to choose to have a cheerful heart instead of a broken spirit. Psychologists know from research and case studies that a positive attitude plays a large part in recovery. Our doctor told us that those patients who have a spiritual dimension seem to go through illness and treatment better than those who don't. Try your best to have a positive attitude daily. Be known as a person with a cheerful heart. Have a smile for those you meet.

Prayer: *Father God, we want to be cheerful today, even*
when we don't feel like it. Help me to lift my
spirits so I can be a blessing for someone who has

a special need. I know that when I give a blessing, I am blessed. Amen.

Action: Buy a joke book and read at least one joke a day. If you are too sick, have someone read it to you.

Reflections:

As Pure as Solid Gold

*He knows every detail of what is happening to me,
and when he has examined me, he will pronounce me
completely innocent—as pure as solid gold!*

—Job 23:10

God knows me so well that He even knows the path I will take in life. He knows from the beginning to the end. The Lord knows those who are His. We each have a will, and He allows us to make our own decisions. Some of those decisions will be like silver and gold and some will be more like wood, hay, or stubble. Some will be honorable, some not. If we will cleanse ourselves of dishonor, we will become a vessel for honor and useful for the Master—prepared for every good work.

It takes a great amount of heat to separate impurities from gold. I have looked upon my trials as a time of refinement. Each time I said to God, *Please stop, it's too hot*, He would answer back, *not yet*. Just think—I will be refined as gold, pure of any imperfections. Gold is a commodity that has remained universally valuable over time. We must be very valuable if He considers us as pure gold.

Prayer: Father God, You are making me as pure as gold. I
              don't understand the process, but I believe in the
              Processor. I am willing to trust You. Amen.

Action: Ask God to show you one impurity He's
              removing from your life.

Reflections:

□ □ □

Be Assured

And don't forget the many times I clearly told you
what was going to happen in the future.
For I am God—I only—and there is no other like me
who can tell you what is going to happen.
All I say will come to pass, for I do whatever I wish.

—Isaiah 46:9-10

s I look at the magazine racks by the checkout stand at my favorite market, I'm amazed at all the prophecy headlines. Everyone wants to be the expert who's going to tell you what's going to happen. No topic is off limits—from the return of Jesus to improving your sex life. As believers, we already have the Expert in our hearts. He knows everything; there is no other. He is awesome. He knows the beginning and the end. He is the keeper of the final events of history. This is God, in whom I put my trust. History has proven that we can trust His words—they are never changing and they fit into His plans for our lives. Be assured that you are at the top of His priority list. Isn't it wonderful to know that you are a part of God's plan?

Prayer: *Father God, I know I can trust Your plan for my life. Even though I may not be able to put the puzzle of life together, You have. I'm willing to trust in You. Amen.*

Action: Live in a way that shows that you are trusting
God's plan for your life.

Reflections:

When the sun is refusing to shine on your day
and you're finding it hard just to cope,
When you're seeing more rain clouds than stars in the sky
and you just feel like giving up hope,
That's the time when someone comes along with a smile
and a warm hug that say, "It's okay—
Tomorrow is coming, so don't give up now—
brighter moments are soon on their way!"

—EMILY MATTHEWS

Be a Woman of Joy

*You have let me experience the joys of life and
the exquisite pleasures of your own eternal presence.*

—Psalm 16:11

Someone once asked Mother Teresa what the job description was for anyone who might wish to work alongside her in the dirty streets, with the stench of human waste and the overflowing of death, in the densely populated city of Calcutta, India. Without even giving a moment's thought she responded:

- The desire to work hard

- A joyful attitude

What great advice for all of us, regardless of where we live. We could live in a mansion or in a cardboard home, and the advice would still be appropriate. If you are willing to work hard and exhibit a joyful attitude, you will be successful in life. One thing I enjoy doing is supporting businesses that exhibit both of these character traits. It's no fun to be around those who are lazy and exhibit no joy. I've also noticed that those who have a lot of friends are those who work hard and have joy. I want to learn these valuable traits from successful people. When I feel down, I want to exhibit joyfulness, and when I feel lazy, I want a new zeal in my body.

Prayer: Father God, let me concentrate on these two traits, so my life will reflect both of them. Amen.

Action: Work hard and enjoy your work.

Reflections:

Receive and Give

❧

I will bless the Lord and not forget
the glorious things he does for me.

—PSALM 103:2

Some say we have two arms because one arm is for receiving and the other arm is for giving. What a balance for life! We don't just want to always receive; we must remember that 50 percent of the time we are to give. I know when I give a gift to someone, I get so excited. I can't wait to see the expression on their face. If a kind word is all you can afford, then give a kind word. It costs nothing but returns great dividends.

Some of the most wonderful greeting cards I have received were handmade by my grandchildren. I set them out so all our guests see them. Everything we have is a gift—our health, hearing, eyesight, mental abilities, jobs, homes—given to us by God. Why waste time reflecting on what we don't have? Let's fill our minds with the things we do have. Negative thoughts destroy; positive thoughts make us full of joy. Learn to give abundantly—your joy will be complete.

Prayer: Father God, you have given me so much; in return, I want to give to others. Let my joy and radiance be a blessing today. Amen.

Action: Give of yourself to others.

Reflections:

No Pain, No Gain

*Happy is the man who doesn't give in
and do wrong when he is tempted, for afterwards
he will get as his reward the crown of life
that God has promised those who love him.*

—JAMES 1:12

ave you ever felt like quitting? I know I
have. I'm not very competitive, so *hanging in
there* is not always in my vocabulary. My
son, who is a triathlete and runs marathons, would tell
me in a small voice, "Mom, no pain, no gain." Just what I
didn't want to hear. My Bob was also a great encourager.
When I was down, he would motivate me to get back up
and try again.

Hang in there—don't let the enemy defeat you. I
know there are many days when you want to run and
hide, but believe me, there is light at the end of the
tunnel. When you first see that light, you will be so glad
that you didn't quit. I am experiencing a quality of life
now that I never thought I would experience. Each new
day is a bouquet of flowers. I no longer take anything for
granted. The smells, the sounds, the touches of what I
used to take for granted are now highlights of my day.
Each day is precious.

Prayer: Father God, you truly are giving me my reward
              for not quitting. I appreciate each 24 hours I have
              to enjoy Your creation. Amen.

Action: Don't give up—look for the ray of light.

Reflections:

Learning a Lesson

❧

Since the Lord is directing our steps,
why try to understand everything
that happens along the way?

—Proverbs 20:24

ut God, are You sure that You meant this trial for me? Didn't You mean for it to go to Bill, Sue, or Jamie? I'm sure You made a mistake when You gave me this illness. Does that kind of thinking sound familiar? I know it crossed my mind once or twice. I honestly didn't want to accept the diagnosis of cancer. Other people get this disease, but not me.

However, after I got over the shock and my emotions and thought process came back to earth, I knew I had two choices: be angry at God, or accept what I was about to go through and realize that this situation was going to make me a better person. Trials are never wasted, nor does God give them to the wrong person. He did *not* give me cancer, but He *did* give me the opportunity to grow as a person during this venture. Through all the pain, tears, hurts, inconveniences, and prayers, we learn to grow and depend upon His Word. Yes, we grow and learn as we cry and pray.

Prayer: Father God, I want to open my heart and learn from the trials I have. However, I struggle at times. My natural self wants to resist these trials. Thank You for understanding my humanness. Amen.

Action: Open your heart's door to trials.

Reflections:

You Must Not Quit

When things go wrong, as they sometimes will,
When the road you're trudging seems all uphill,
When the funds are low and the debts are high,
And you want to smile but you have to sigh,
When care is pressing you down a bit,
Rest if you must, but don't you quit.

Life is strange with its twists and turns
As every one of us sometimes learns;
And many a failure turns about
When he might have won had he stuck it out.
Don't give up though the pace seems slow;
You may succeed with another blow!

Success is failure turned inside out,
The silver tint of the clouds of doubt;
And you never can tell just how close you are,
It may be near when it seems so far.
So stick to the fight when you're hardest hit;
When things seem worst, you must not quit.

—Author Unknown

The Lesson of the Locusts

❧

If I command the locust swarms
to eat up all your crops...

—2 Chronicles 7:13

Have you ever felt that your life was being pared down to the bare essentials? That's what the experience of cancer can be like. So can a number of other experiences: a bereavement, a serious accident, a divorce, a job loss. Even a passage like an empty nest or retirement can allow troubles to move in like swarming locusts on a grain field and strip your life of everything you care about.

That's certainly what the past five years have felt like for me. One loss after another—the trivial with the large—until I almost couldn't recognize the landscape of my life.

I don't know why, but I never asked God, "Why me?" I think it's because I know very well my locust years are nothing special—others have experienced much worse than I have.

What have I learned? First of all, that the damage is real. The losses we sustain during our stripping-down times are significant. The restored life God gives us to make up for the lost locust years is much better in some ways than the life we had before, but it will never be the same. The beauty of divine restoration is that God can and does use the very circumstances of our losses to shape our lives. God's love continues through our losses.

Prayer: Father God, let me look beyond the present and look forward to the restoration years. You are a God of redemption, and I thank You for restoring what the locust has eaten. Amen.

Action: Take a moment and meditate about how God is still in control.

Reflections:

Just You Wait

🍂

I wait for the Lord, my soul waits, and in his word
I put my hope. My soul waits for the Lord
more than watchmen wait for the morning.

—PSALM 130:5-6 NIV

I knew cancer would be a difficult experience. But I wasn't quite prepared for just how tedious an experience it would be!

The waiting has been the hardest part of my cancer years. That's not surprising, because waiting is one of the hardest things all of us have to do in our lives. It's an unavoidable part of being human. We should not be surprised that so many passages in the Bible speak about enduring and being patient.

When things are going well, we wait for them to get better. When times are hard, we wait for circumstances to improve. We wait for good things in anticipation and frustration. And when we are ill or in trouble, the waiting can be simply excruciating. Jesus said that in this world we would have trouble. He didn't specifically add that a lot of our trouble would involve waiting.

Why is waiting so hard? Sometimes we're in a hurry because we want the outcome so badly. We just have to know. Another reason waiting is hard is that it takes away our illusion of control. Our spirits rebel against this reminder that our time is not our own—a lot of what happens is out-side our power and control.

Prayer: *Father God, let me use this waiting time to develop my trust in You. I don't have to know all the answers just now. I can learn to wait on You! Amen.*

Action: When all you can do is wait, lean on the promises of God.

Reflections:

The Cupboard's Not Bare

Don't store up treasures here on earth
where they can erode away or may be stolen.
Store them in heaven where they will never lose
their value, and are safe from thieves.

—MATTHEW 6:19-20

Remember that sad old nursery rhyme about poor Mother Hubbard and her hungry dog? She went to fetch him a bone, but when she got there the cupboard was bare.

I know a little bit about empty cupboards. I grew up in a home where my mother worked day and night to keep body and soul together. And while she always managed to feed us, there were times when our tiny apartment cupboard held little more than a few potatoes and a box of Earl Grey tea.

Maybe that's why I've always loved the idea of a well-stocked, well-organized cupboard. I'm not talking literally about my pantry; I'm talking about physical, emotional, and spiritual provisions that can carry you through difficult times. This would include building good friendships, developing a spiritual foundation that gives you hope regarding God's plans for your life, and trusting in God's word to keep you from high stress and worry. These are pantry staples that have eternal values. They will not rust or rot away.

I can see clearly now that the Lord was stocking my cupboards with the physical, emotional, and spiritual resources I would need to survive my cancer years.

Prayer: *Father God, thank You for giving me a good shopping list for my cupboards—items that won't rust or rot away. Amen.*

Action: Take stock of your physical, emotional, and spiritual provisions.

Reflections:

Cancerland

How can we sing the LORD's song
in a foreign land?

—PSALM 137:4 NASB

'm not the first person to call it Cancerland. Others before me have noticed that undergoing cancer treatment is a little like journeying through a foreign country where everything is different from what you're used to.

The scenery is strange—largely limited to waiting rooms, therapy rooms, sofas, beds, and the narrow path between home, the doctor's office, and the emergency room. But there are moments when the vista widens to show you amazing things about God's truth and the human spirit you would otherwise never have glimpsed.

The best thing about Cancerland is that it's full of good people. If you travel there, you'll meet a number of medical professionals, an assortment of fellow tourists (many in scarves and wigs), and a number of friends and family members who come along as companions on the journey.

And although the land feels foreign to me, God lives there, too. He has sustained me and my family during our journey.

Now I can see what I couldn't see in the beginning: God is working in all of us, building new strength and flexibility into our characters, teaching us to trust and obey, and encouraging us to thank Him in every circumstance.

Prayer: *Father God, You are so amazing. Even when I go to a foreign land, You are there beside me. What an encouragement You have been! Amen.*

Action: Fear not—God is with you in Cancerland.

Reflections:

Cancer is so limited…
It cannot cripple love.
It cannot shatter hope.
It cannot corrode faith.
It cannot eat away peace.
It cannot destroy confidence.
It cannot kill friendship.
It cannot shut out memories.
It cannot silence courage.
It cannot invade the soul.
It cannot steal eternal life.
It cannot quench the Spirit.
It cannot lessen the power of resurrection.

—AUTHOR UNKNOWN

The Big Picture

❧

The joy of the Lord is your strength.

—NEHEMIAH 8:10

In the big picture, joy will prevail over sadness because God has won His ultimate battle over the forces of evil. Everything that happens now is just a matter of cleaning up. That's the big picture that makes comfort and joy appropriate and possible even in the face of great evil, suffering, and pain.

Because of what God has done and is doing in the world and in my life, I can really take comfort. Because He has the last word, I can rejoice—not because of my suffering, but in the midst of it. And because He is always present and working in my life, I can celebrate even as I mourn. I can rejoice in my suffering because I know God is working through it to strengthen me and build my character. I can rejoice in spite of my suffering because of what I know God is doing behind the scenes—bringing about my hopeful future. That's the big picture.

Rejoicing will sometimes be difficult and challenging. Comfort will sometimes be hard to find. We not only need to understand all will be well, but we also need to convince our hearts, souls, and spirits of this joyful reality.

Prayer: Father God, let real joy be a reality in my life.
             Allow me to make it a realization in my life today.
             Amen.

Action: Write down your main sources of comfort
             and consolation.

Reflections:

Rejoice in the Lord

Always be full of joy in the Lord;
I say it again, rejoice!

—PHILIPPIANS 4:4

To be honest with you, I didn't like having cancer. The symptoms were frightening, annoying, and sometimes excruciating. The treatment was no fun at all. The side effects and related syndromes—such as shingles—I could happily have lived without. I wasn't wild about the way the disease overturned and rearranged my life, and I really hated the long, dark, worrisome nights.

The truth is, there's nothing inherently uplifting about a life-destroying disease. Given the choice, I'd just as soon have avoided the whole thing. So if you ask me whether my cancer journey was a joyful or comforting experience, I'd have to say no. But if you ask me whether I experienced comfort and joy during those five years, my answer would be different. For even in the midst of fear, pain, and occasional despair, the comfort was real, the joy unmistakable, and the hope unshaken.

Prayer: Father God, let me reflect your joy and hope even in the midst of my suffering. I can see the big picture and know that I have victory. Thank You. Amen.

Action: Rejoice and trust in your suffering.

Reflections:

Back from the Grave

✿

O Lord my God, I pleaded with you,
and you gave me my health again.
You brought me back from the brink of the grave,
from death itself, and here I am alive!

—PSALM 30:2-3

Have you ever asked yourself the question, *What do I know for sure?* When I ask myself that probing question in terms of my bout with cancer, a couple of things come to mind.

One thing I know is that God is good. That has become our family's motto: God is Good. We knew it before, but now we really know it. Even when circumstances seemed unbearable, the Lord's goodness kept shining through. In each ordeal, we felt the bedrock reality of God's goodness underneath us.

And I know that God heals. I know this not just because I've read it in the Bible or met others who have been healed. I know this because He has worked a miracle of healing in my life. It came about a little differently than I expected, and took a lot longer than I thought it would, but it was still a bona fide, praise-worthy, hallelujah-inspiring miracle.

God heals. I believe that with all my heart. And I have also come to believe healing is a process we can't always understand. Only God knows.

Prayer: Father God, I praise You for my healing. You are a
mysterious God who has a plan for each of our
lives. May I praise Your name with the life I have.
Amen.

Action: Trust God for your miracle.

Reflections:

Become the Body of Christ

*Whatever you did for one of the least of these
brothers of mine, you did for me.*

—MATTHEW 25:40 NIV

id you know that Jesus lives in cancer clinics?
I know it's true because I've seen Him there.
I've heard His voice. I've felt His tender
touch, even during the most frightening moments of my
treatment.

Our Lord walks the corridors with a bald head and puffy
face, with scars from surgery and IV drips hanging from His
arms. Sometimes He wears a hospital badge and a clinician's
coat. Sometimes He sits in waiting rooms or keeps watch at
bedsides.

His hands are the hands that scrub bathrooms, or make
soup, or copy Scripture onto a notecard. His feet are the feet
that make rounds or mow the grass for someone else. His
eyes are the eyes that notice needs and attend to them. He
speaks love over long-distance lines. His heart shines from
handwritten cards and hastily typed emails.

> Christ has no body now but yours; no hands,
> no feet on earth, but yours.
> Yours are the eyes through which He looks
> with compassion on this world;
> Yours are the feet with which He walks to do
> good;

Yours are the hands with which He blesses
all the world.
Christ has no body now on earth but yours.

—TERESA OF AVILA

Through the hands, feet, eyes, and hearts of so many of God's people, I received the blessing of God's care during my illness.

Prayer: *Father God, fellow Christians have been Your feet, hands, heart, and soul during my illness. Thanks for the working body of Christ. Amen.*

Action: Go out and be a representative of Jesus.

Reflections:

In the end we shall find every promise of God
perfectly fulfilled. Then why should we not let
our hearts rest in peace about everything that happens?
Nothing can happen that can break a single one
of these precious promises. There is no promise
of an easy passage, but there are promises
for every day of the voyage. Each day let us take one
promise for our own, live on it, test
and prove it—and thank God for it.

—AMY CARMICHAEL

God Is Listening

O Lord God! You have made the heavens and earth
by your great power; nothing is too hard for you!

—JEREMIAH 32:17

I don't know why I even try to understand God with my tiny brain. He is so much greater than I am. I stand in awe when I journey to the mountains, the desert, or the beach, and see all of His creations. When I feel the rumble of the earthquakes here in southern California, or witness the mighty forces of hurricanes and tornadoes, I can scarcely comprehend the power of His creation. He truly is awesome, and I know He can do anything!

But even though I can't always understand Him, I do trust Him to do what He has promised. I pray that God's will might be done in my life and that I will be able to hear and accept His direction. And I ask for added days to my life—if it fits in His plan—I know He can do that, too!

Prayer: *Father God, I petition for added days in my life. You are the Giver of life, thus I ask You to heal my body from this disease. With this extension, I will glorify You forever and ever. Amen.*

Action: Pray to God today for a healing. Keep on keeping on.

Reflections:

Be a Blessing

Be kind to each other, tenderhearted,
forgiving one another, just as God has forgiven you
because you belong to Christ.

—EPHESIANS 4:32

I am so thankful for all of my kind and compassionate friends. The outpouring of love I have experienced the past few years has absolutely astonished me. Cards, letters, candies, flowers, and faxes have flowed from friends, family, and even those who know me only from my books and seminars. I have learned so much about love and caring from these people who have shown me such amazing kindness and compassion.

But the people who have forgiven me my faults and failings are the ones who leave me really humbled—friends and family who sometimes become the target of my cross moods or critical spirit. Planners of meetings I have had to cancel, phone friends who understand unreturned calls, gracious acquaintances who answer my apologies with smiling good grace. It is the forgiveness of others that reminds me of how much my heavenly Father forgives me—and how important cultivating the art of forgiveness in my own heart is. Forgiveness works at a soul level and eventually changes everything—beginning with the heart of the forgiver.

Prayer: Father God, You have forgiven me, so I can forgive others. Reveal to me those that need forgiveness. My soul wants to be at peace with all those that I may have offended. Amen.

Action: Set your slate clean—forgive those that need forgiveness.

Reflections:

The Eyes of the Lord

Pity me, O Lord, for I am weak.
Heal me, for my body is sick.

—PSALM 6:2

A young man, Glenn Baxley, after reading my book *Fill My Cup, Lord,* sat down and wrote these words:

The eyes of the Lord are upon me
For I love Him
He will take care of my each and every need
I'll be encouraged through hardship
I'll revere Him
I have all that I desire
For you see
The eyes of the Lord
Are forever upon me.

Lord, You are my hope
When my spirit's weak
I know You're with the brokenhearted
Those who will believe
I will trust You
You encourage me
I have no fear of what's ahead of me
*The eyes of the Lord are forever upon me.**

---

* Used by permission.

These words were later put to music. What an honor to be a part of the inspiration that created this beautiful song. Glenn's wife had left him, and he didn't know where to turn. He was lonely and heartbroken because of this separation. At the bottom of his emotional curve, he turned to the safety of the Lord. His words became my words: *He will take care of my each and every need.* Fellow reader, no matter where you are in life, these words are for you. Hold tight and trust God for delivery from every situation. God is watching over you.

Prayer: *Father God, I'm so glad Your eyes are upon me each and every day. You are my hope. I have no fear of what's ahead of me. Amen.*

Action: Incorporate the words of this song into your life.

Reflections:

A Secure Future

🌾

He will wipe away all tears from their eyes,
and there shall be no more death, nor sorrow,
nor crying, nor pain. All of that has gone forever.

—Revelation 21:4

Isn't it wonderful to know the big picture? When we know that God is working in our lives, we can relax and be at peace with whatever comes our way. Let me share a few verses that helped me relax with my final destiny—whatever it may be:

- ❧ He will swallow up death forever. The Lord God will wipe away all tears… (Isaiah 25:8).

- ❧ Your sun shall never set; the moon shall not go down—for the Lord will be your everlasting light; your days of mourning all will end (Isaiah 60:20).

- ❧ And I will rejoice in Jerusalem, and in my people; and the voice of weeping and crying shall not be heard there any more (Isaiah 65:19).

- ❧ All sorrow and all sighing will be gone forever; only joy and gladness will be there (Isaiah 35:10).

- ❧ O Death, bring forth your terrors for his tasting! O Grave, demonstrate your plagues! For I will not relent (Hosea 13:14).

- ❧ The last enemy that will be abolished is death (1 Corinthians 15:26 NASB).

- ❧ Death is swallowed up in victory (1 Corinthians 15:54 NASB).

The big picture is that Jesus will conquer the sting of death. As believers, we will be with Him forever secure in our future.

Prayer: *Father God, I thank You for sharing with me the victory we all have over death. If this disease ends in death, I know that I will have victory over it. What peace and comfort You give. Amen.*

Action: Find big victories in small things.

Reflections:

---

*Now unto Him that is able to do
exceeding abundantly above all that we ask or think,
according to the power that worketh in us...*

—EPHESIANS 3:20 KJV

Other Minute Meditations™ Books
by Bob & Emilie Barnes

ᘒ ᘒ ᘒ

Minute Meditations™ for Couples
Bob & Emilie Barnes

Giving you quick opportunities to draw near to God—and each other—these inspiring quotes, encouraging words, and practical advice reflect the deep bonds trials spark in couples committed to each other.

Minute Meditations™ for Busy Moms
Emilie Barnes

Time-challenged moms get encouragement and direction for reflecting Christ in their homes and beyond. Short prayers and action steps help you put challenging notions into motion. A prayerful pick-me-up for mothers on the go.

Minute Meditations™ for Women
Emilie Barnes

Encouraging you to seek the Lord in every circumstance, these 5-minute readings offer gentle insights and Scripture to highlight the joys of sharing Jesus, encouraging husbands, becoming children of God, and more.

Minute Meditations™ for Men
Bob Barnes

Is finding meaningful time with God possible with all the demands on your time? Yes. These two- and three-minute meditations, packed with encouragement, will make an incredible difference in how you handle the day's pressures and maximize your time with God.

Other Harvest House Books
by Bob & Emilie Barnes

🐝 🐝 🐝

Books by
Bob & Emilie Barnes

*Minute Meditations™
for Couples*

*A Little Book of Manners
for Boys*

Abundance of the Heart

*15 Minute Devotions
for Couples*

Books by Emilie Barnes

The 15-Minute Organizer

15 Minutes Alone with God

*15 Minutes of Peace
with God*

101 Ways to Lift Your Spirits

*The Busy Woman's Guide
to Healthy Eating*

A Tea to Comfort Your Soul

A Cup of God's Love

A Cup of Hope

*Emilie's Creative
Home Organizer*

*Everything I Know
I Learned from My Garden*

Fill My Cup, Lord

Friends Are a Blessing

Friends of the Heart

Help Me Trust You, Lord

If Teacups Could Talk

An Invitation to Tea

Join Me for Tea

A Journey Through Cancer

*Keep It Simple
for Busy Women*

Let's Have a Tea Party!

A Little Book of Manners

*Minute Meditations™
for Busy Moms*

*Minute Meditations™
for Women*

More Hours in My Day

Safe in the Father's Hands

*Strength for Today,
Bright Hope for Tomorrow*

Survival for Busy Women

*The Twelve Teas®
of Celebration*

*The Twelve Teas®
of Christmas*

*The Twelve Teas®
of Friendship*

Books by Bob Barnes

*15 Minutes Alone with God
for Men*

Minute Meditations™ for Men

*What Makes a Man
Feel Loved*